Blueprint 2050

Sustaining the Marine Environment in Mainland Tanzania and Zanzibar

THE WORLD BANK
Washington, D.C.

Photographs: by courtesy of Paavo Eliste, Claudio Georgette, Aaron Hamerlynck, Indu Hewawasam and Dean Housden. Cover, graphic designs and illustrations by Gelise McCullough; cover photos based on composites courtesy of Paavo Eliste and Indu Hewawasam. Chapter cover graphics based on photos of khangas by Gelise McCullough.

ISBN 0-8213-6123-6

Library of Congress Cataloging-in-Publication Data has been applied for.

Ruitenbeek, Jack 1958–
Hewawasam, Indu 1953–
Ngoile, Magnus 1949–
Blueprint 2050: Sustaining the marine environment in mainland Tanzania and Zanzibar/ Jack Ruitenbeek, Indu Hewawasam, Magnus Ngoile, editors.
                              21x24 cm
Includes bibliographical references. Includes CD insert.
ISBN: 0-8213-6123-6
  1. Marine protected areas – Tanzania. 2. Poverty alleviation – Tanzania. I. Title.

Contents

Statement from the Vice President's Office

THE UNITED REPUBLIC OF TANZANIA

VICE-PRESIDENT'S OFFICE

P.O. BOX 5380

DAR ES SALAAM

TANZANIA

Blueprint 2050 provides us with an opportunity for reflection and strategic visioning on the sustainable use of our coastal and marine resources which are vital to the economy of Tanzania. Twenty-five percent of our country's population live in coastal areas, sharing with them some of the most diverse and biologically important species on earth such as the coelacanth and dugong.

Tanzania's coastal resources are under increasing pressure; unless immediate measures are taken these resources will not support future coastal communities. We – the present generation – have a duty to ensure that the coastal and marine resources contribute to the livelihoods of the coastal people (especially to the poorest of the poor) and to the economy of the country, while at the same time conserving these resources for future Tanzanians. This requires maintaining a critical balance between use and conservation.

Establishing a system of marine protected areas (MPAs) is the path to success in sustaining the critical balance. Tanzania is committed to ensuring that 10 percent of its coastal and marine areas will be under MPAs by 2012 and 20 percent by 2025. Every support must be mobilized to achieve this goal and the vision set out in Blueprint 2050. It is partly for this reason that the Government of Tanzania is initiating the Marine and Coastal Environment Management Project (MACEMP).

Hon Raphael OS Mollel

Senior Permanent Secretary

Vice President's Office

United Republic of Tanzania

Foreword

Since the 1992 "Earth Summit" in Rio de Janeiro, countries have become much more aware of the need to protect and manage their marine resources. They realize that it's not just about creating wealth today, but about ensuring that marine resources are protected for future generations. For many developing countries, fisheries and marine products provide major opportunities for promoting economic growth. At the same time it is these countries that are least able to enforce regulations, prevent over-fishing and protect their marine resources.

The 2003 World Parks Congress in Durban confirmed that, if managed properly, marine resources offer enormous potential for effective wealth creation and poverty reduction. Policy makers worldwide have committed to using marine protected areas as a mechanism for promoting resource management while improving economic well-being.

Policy makers in Tanzania outline targets for growth and poverty reduction in the draft National Strategy for Growth and Reduction of Poverty. These combined with the UN's 2015 Millennium Development Goals can be achieved and maintained only through sustainable use of Tanzania's natural resources, including its marine resources.

The Tanzanian authorities have started to involve local communities in decisions about managing marine resources and sharing in their economic benefits as part of a broader community driven approach to development. The importance of coastal communities' indigenous knowledge is also increasingly appreciated by policy makers.

The World Bank has mainstreamed environmental concerns into its overall poverty reduction goals. In Tanzania this commitment is evidenced in a variety of ways: analytical work, partnerships, and financing of the Government budget, as well as environmental programs, including the planned Marine and Coastal Environment Management Project (MACEMP). The MACEMP aims to strengthen institutional capacity of Tanzania to enforce policies with a positive impact on coastal populations and has the potential for setting in place the blueprint for sound management of marine and coastal resources throughout East Africa.

This book provides an important contribution to the national – and regional – dialog on marine protected area management. It provides an unusually long time horizon, 50 years, and challenges us to take action today, given the long gestation of many environmental actions.

The Bank remains a committed development partner to Tanzania in the sustainable use of its coastal and marine resources.

Judy O'Connor

Country Director for Tanzania

Africa Region – World Bank

Preface

We present this as an "edited" volume in the hopes that we can fairly acknowledge the diversity of inputs that contributed to the findings and recommendations contained herein. But it is not an edited volume in the conventional sense of a collection of distinct papers with distinct conclusions. It is, by contrast, an edited volume of numerous ideas and findings – some explicitly formulated, others not. The contributors to those ideas and findings range from technical experts to government officials to private sector investors to marine park managers to local fishermen and their families. The ideas and findings are not always completely in agreement with each other, and in such cases we have tried to offer both (or more!) sides of the story, or proffered a middle ground based on our own experience and interpretations. We thus walk a fine line between authors and editors, but we do so with the utmost respect for the positions of all of those who might rightfully be regarded as co-authors of this work. On some occasions we found ourselves taking an idea – such as that for pooled financing or for firmer community access to near shore waters – and turning it into something as concrete as a "Marine Legacy Fund" or a "Community Territorial Sea." The names we attach to these concepts are not so important in the long term; what is meaningful is that they came from concepts and ideas that have emerged from hundreds of conversations, workshops, meetings and writings – either within the context of this project or through related activities. We are sincerely grateful to all of those who in some way contributed to those concepts and ideas, and hope that – in reading this book – they will see how we have turned their thoughts into a potential vision for marine and coastal protection and sustainable use over the coming decades.

Chapter Covers

Zanzibari sayings and metaphors are known worldwide and come about from a long tradition of making witty and wise observations on day-to-day matters. Many of these sayings find their way to writings on locally worn khangas or (more recently) tee-shirts. Khangas are colourful rectangles of cloth that are customarily used as clothing, for carrying infant children, or for decorative purposes such as table cloths or wall hangings. The chapter covers in this book – designed by Gelise McCullough – show some typical khanga motifs and include, within each one, a Swahili saying that intends to introduce or capture key messages in the respective chapters. The editors are also grateful to Zainab Semgalawe for assistance in selecting and interpreting these sayings. Their meanings can be interpreted as follows:

Chapter 1: Mtembezi hula miguu yake. "An aimless wanderer wears away his feet."

Chapter 2: Maji usiyoyafika hujui kina chake. "You cannot tell the depth of water you have never been into."

Chapter 3: Furaha ya mvuvi nafuu kwa mchukuzi. "When the fishermen are happy, the porters are happy too."

Chapter 4: Kumla nguru si kazi, kazi kumwosha. "It is no trouble to eat a kingfish, the trouble lies in cleaning it."

Chapter 5: Mvuvi anajua pweza alipo. "A fisherman knows where to look for an octopus."

Chapter 6: Penye wengi hapaharibiki neno. "Where there are many people, nothing goes wrong."

Photo Claudio Georgette

The main inputs into this book have come from a comprehensive in-country process and, similarly, the primary audience for this book remains this same in-country process. The process is very real and tangible. Efforts to increase community participation in coastal resource management, efforts to improve protection of the territorial seas, and efforts to manage the risks associated with increased development and population pressures are all continuing apace on the Tanzania mainland and the Zanzibar islands. This volume is intended to inform these efforts, and to provide options for moving forward. It is not intended as a prescriptive recipe that guaranties success. Indeed, there will likely be a fair share of successes and failures as the process continues; such is the nature of an adaptive learning process. To date, however, we would judge that the process has been a success, and much of this success is because of the dedication of those who have provided their intellect, experience and insight to the work herein.

Foremost, we are thankful for the strong political will and support that has characterized the entire process. We thank Hon Madam Zakia Meghji, Minister of Natural Resources and Tourism, and Hon Arcado Ntagazwa, Minister of State for Environment, for their political commitment to addressing the critical issues in marine and coastal areas and for their support for the technical studies. We are grateful to Hon Madam Rahma M Mshangama, Principal Secretary MANREC Zanzibar, who hosted the May 2004 Zanzibar workshop and provided important leadership throughout the discussions. We thank Hon Solomon Odunga, Permanent Secretary of MNRT for his consistent support throughout the implementation of the technical studies. And we are grateful that Hon Raphael OS Mollel, Senior Permanent Secretary of the Vice President's Office of the United Republic of Tanzania, has endorsed this process and its findings.

This book relies extensively on a series of scientific and technical studies conducted in 2003 and 2004.[1] Contributors to these background studies include: ecology – Sue Wells, Saada Juma, Chris Muhando, Vedast Makota, and Tundi Agardy; socio-economics and poverty – Yolanda León, James Tobey, Elin Torell, Rose Mwaipopo, Adolfo Mkenda, Zainab Ngazy, Farhat Mbarouk, Paavo Eliste and Patricia Silva; cultural issues – Karen Moon; financial sustainability and economics – Andrew Hurd, Henrik Lindhjem, and Jack Ruitenbeek; legal – Vincent Shauri. Bernice Mclean conducted some of the initial research that was used in the grant proposal to define these research needs.

Important insights were received during a workshop in Zanzibar in May 2004 as part of preparatory activities for the World Bank and Global Environment Facility supported Marine and Coastal Environment Management Project (MACEMP). The workshop included some 60 participants from various levels of government, from the donor community, from the private sector, and from civil society and non-governmental organizations. Many of the facts and ideas in this book were elaborated, verified, and further developed during this workshop; the open and frank discussions contributed immeasurably to the conclusions, and we sincerely thank those who engaged in the discourse.

We would like to extend a special thank you to all of those individuals who provided specific feedback on an extensive questionnaire that was meant to act as a reality check on some of the key conclusions in this book. The questionnaire involved some two dozen questions ranging across complex technical topics as well as politically sensitive issues; the time and care that was taken by so many people in responding to this questionnaire is testimony to their dedication to improving the welfare of coastal inhabitants. Within government, we especially thank: Amin Abdallah (Marine Parks and Reserves Unit), Bakari Asseid (Director, Department of Commercial Crops, Fruits and Forestry, Zanzibar), Philemon Luhanjo (Permanent Secretary, Ministry of Foreign Affairs), R Mapunda (Acting Director, Fisheries Department MNRT), Josephine Meela (Senior Environmental Management Officer, National

---

1. Background studies are available in electronic format on the enclosed CD or upon request to the authors.

Environmental Management Council), Amani Ngusaru (Coordinator, East African Marine Ecoregion Program), AM Othman (Manager, Menai Bay Conservation Area), Salim Ammar Salim (Chief Fisheries Officer, Fisheries Department MANREC), CR Rumisha (Head, Marine Parks and Reserves Unit), and Issa Suleiman (Fisheries Officer, Artisanal Fisheries, MANREC).

In addition, we extend our thanks to Jim Anderson, Ian Christie, Gary Graig, Marea Hatziolos, Andy Hooten, Melanie Marlett, Matt Richmond, Jason Rubens, and Robert Townsend for sharing with us their insights and experience.

The authors acknowledge the kind permission of IUCN - The World Conservation Union and the Rufiji Environmental Management Project for consent to summarize an article relating to the Brushwood Parks in Tanzania. Contributors to the original article included Olivier Hamerlynck, Rose Hogan, Matt Richmond and Anne de Villiers. We also thank IUCN for their ongoing support and feedback throughout the project as a whole; Melita Samoilys and Abdulrahman Issa of the IUCN East Africa Regional Office in Nairobi provided key review comments relating to ecological elements. At IUCN Headquarters, special thanks go to Joshua Bishop and Carl-Gustav Lundin for their feedback on earlier writings and for hosting a seminar in Gland, Switzerland in June 2004 at which the key conclusions and recommendations of Blueprint 2050 were discussed further. Among the discussants were participants from World Wildlife Fund including Sarah Humphrey (WWF International, Gland) and Sam Kanyamibwa (WWF Eastern Africa Regional Programme Office, Nairobi), who provided useful critique and feedback based on their experience.

Finally, we are grateful to David Freestone and Ron Zweig, who provided useful peer review comments on earlier drafts of the manuscript.

Financing for this book, the background studies, and related activities was provided by the Environmentally Socially Sustainable Development Trust Fund under Grant #TF051421.

We are also grateful to Zainab Semgalawe for her assistance with selecting and interpreting the khanga sayings that adorn the chapter cover graphics. Aza Rashid and Gloria Sindano provided valuable assistance in organizing the numerous consultative meetings, workshops and interviews that contributed to this book. Dean Housden coordinated collaborative efforts with the Office of the Publisher.

In the production of this book, we are grateful for the additional editorial assistance from Cynthia Cartier. Layout and graphics of the book were prepared by Gelise McCullough. Maps were prepared by Vedast Makota and Chris Muhando based on digital information provided by the National Environment Management Council and the Institute of Marine Sciences (University of Dar es Salaam).

The book is being published under the leadership of Karen Brooks, Sector Manager, Environment, Rural and Social Development Operations, East Africa, Africa Region.

Jack Ruitenbeek

Indu Hewawasam

Magnus Ngoile

About the Editors

Indu Hewawasam is Senior Environmental Specialist, Environment, Rural and Social Development Operations, East Africa, Africa Region. Since July 2002, she has been based in the World Bank Tanzania Country Office, Dar es Salaam, to manage the World Bank marine and coastal activities in Tanzania, Zanzibar, and Mozambique. Her professional interests include marine policy and integrated coastal management.

Contact: <ihewawasam@worldbank.org>

Magnus Ngoile is Director General of the National Environmental Management Council; he is based in Dar es Salaam, Tanzania. He was Director of the Institute of Marine Sciences (Zanzibar) from 1988 to 1995 and his current professional interest is to incorporate sound environmental scientific analysis into practical development policy prescriptions.

Contact: <mngoile@nemtz.org>/<mngoile@simbanet.net>

Jack Ruitenbeek is a private economic and financial consultant to the World Bank and IUCN; he is based in Divonne-les-Bains, France. His professional interests are in the areas of coastal zone management, protected area management, and complex system design.

Contact: <hjr@island.net>

The editors dedicate this book to the victims and all those affected by the tragic events of 26 December 2004, when an earthquake near Sumatra Indonesia precipitated a tidal wave that wrecked havoc in coastal areas throughout the Indian Ocean basin. At press time (January 2005), over 150,000 individuals were counted among the dead in thirteen affected nations.

Photo Dean Housden

Abbreviations

ACM	Adaptive Co-management
AIGA	Alternative Income Generating Activity
ASCA	Accumulated Savings and Credit Association
BIEA	British Institute in East Africa
BMU	Beach Management Unit
CCC	Central Coordinating Committee (Tanga Program)
CHICOP	Chumbe Island Coral Park Ltd.
CITES	Convention on International Trade in Endangered Species
DCCFF	Department of Commercial Crops, Fruits and Forestry (Zanzibar)
DSFA	Deep Sea Fishing Authority
EACC	East African Coastal Current
EAME	East African Marine Ecoregion
EEZ	Exclusive Economic Zone
EIA	Environmental Impact Assessment
EU	European Union
GDP	Gross Domestic Product
GEF	Global Environment Facility
GMP	General Management Plan
IBA	Important Bird Area
ICM	Integrated Coastal Management
IMS	Institute of Marine Sciences (Zanzibar)
IUCN	The World Conservation Union
IUCN EARO	Eastern African Regional Office of the International Union for the Conservation of Nature
KICAMP	Kinondoni Integrated Coastal Area Management Program
LGA	Local Government Act
LME	Large Marine Ecosystem
MACEMP	Marine and Coastal Environment Management Project
MANREC	Ministry of Agriculture, Natural Resources, Environment and Co-operatives

MBCA	Menai Bay Conservation Area
MB-REMP	Mnazi Bay – Ruvuma Estuary Marine Park
MCU	Marine Conservation Unit
MDC	Mafia District Council
MDG	Millennium Development Goal
MICA	Misali Island Conservation Association
MIMCA	Mnemba Island Marine Conservation Area
MIMP	Mafia Island Marine Park
MMA	Marine Management Area
MNRT	Ministry of Natural Resources and Tourism
MP	Marine Park
MPA	Marine Protected Area
MPRA	Marine Parks and Reserves Act
MPRU	Marine Parks and Reserves Unit, Government of Tanzania
MR	Marine Reserve
NGO	Non Governmental Organization
NICEMS	National Integrated Coastal Environment Management Strategy
SAMP	Special Area Management Plan
SEA	Strategic Environmental Assessment
TANAPA	Tanzania National Parks (Authority)
TCMP	Tanzania Coastal Management Partnership
TCZCDP	Tanga Coastal Zone Conservation and Development Program
UNCLOS	United Nations Convention on the Law of the Sea
UNDP	United Nations Development Program
UNEP	United Nations Environmental Program
UNESCO	United Nations Educational, Scientific and Cultural Organization
URT	United Republic of Tanzania
VAT	Value Added Tax
WIO	Western Indian Ocean
WWF	World Wide Fund for Nature
1 US$	1100 Tanzania Shillings (end-2004)

1

THE VISION

Mtembezi hula miguu yake

At the World Parks Congress in Durban in September 2003, URT announced its intention to increase protection of its seas to 10 percent by 2012 and 20 percent by 2025.

Blueprint 2050

Tanzania's territorial seas – comprising 37 000 km² in area and 1 424 km of coastline – are under constant threat from pollution, over-fishing, and destructive development. At the time of writing, only about 1 380 km² of the seas around Tanzania and Zanzibar enjoy some form of protection. Pressure on this ecosystem threatens the long-term livelihoods of the 8 million people that inhabit the country's coastal districts. These people are among the poorest in the country, and are exceedingly vulnerable to man-made and natural shocks that arise in the coastal areas.

This book sets out a Vision for protecting and managing sustainably 100 percent of the seas and coastline on which Tanzania and Zanzibar depend, ensuring that future generations can continue to benefit from the bounty of the resources in the coastal region. The Vision is based on the best available science, drawing from state-of-the-art ecological, socio-economic, financial and institutional studies undertaken explicitly within the context of the United Republic of Tanzania (URT).

We regard this Vision as a Blueprint for the next 50 years or longer, that can be used to guide decision makers, investors, civil society, and other national and regional partners in development and conservation. This Vision is not a cookbook. To the contrary, it promotes a relatively flexible framework that uses a diversity of means to achieve a commonality of purpose. The commonality of purpose is relatively simple:

> *to protect and manage the coastal and marine ecosystems of the United Republic of Tanzania in an ecologically, socially and financially sustainable fashion that alleviates poverty and respects the political and institutional realities in the URT.*

The diversity of means through which this goal is realized is multi-faceted. No ecosystem type, district, institution, or management model is emphasized within this Vision. This is because the starting point is rather complex and itself dictates that a cookie-cutter approach can not be adopted. For example, as a point of departure, we note a number of circumstances that make Tanzania stand out:

- URT is home to some of the most successful models of marine park site management in the world, yet most of the coastal area has no protection at all. Implementation capacity and experience across these areas is thus quite mixed. A diversity of models is required in such situations.

- Two distinct institutional regimes co-exist for the Tanzania mainland and Zanzibar. Management models must respect these and be permitted to emerge based on local needs.

- URT is dedicated to decentralizing its political structures with a view to improving local empowerment, reducing poverty, and improving sustainable resource use. Decentralized decision-making inevitably leads to different structures that cater to local needs.

- Significant scientific uncertainty remains because of lack of information about many of the ecosystems, especially under conditions of global change. Over a long period, systems must be flexible enough to adapt to changes in circumstances, using best available knowledge and techniques at any point in time.

- Vulnerability of human and natural populations – because of inherent poverty or risks associated with global change – is pronounced throughout the coastal area. In such circumstances, safety nets and redundant systems using multiple means reduce vulnerability and provide greater chances of security.

Why do we choose 2050? First, the time scale of ecological systems is generally one with very long cycles. The East African Marine Ecoregion (EAME) programme, for example, has a 50 year time horizon. A long-term view is thus appropriate. From a demographic perspective, we note that Tanzania's population will have more than doubled by then if it continues to grow at recent historical rates (just under 2 percent annually); the dependency on the resource base will also at least double. From an economic perspective, four decades of economic growth at recent levels (approximately 5 percent annually) would imply that Tanzania is a middle income country by 2050; GDP would be almost ten times what it is today, and pressures on resources are historically strongly correlated to economic output. So by planning for 2050, we in fact have in mind that we are planning for double the dependency, and potential impacts that are an order of magnitude higher than what they are today. Fortunately, the increased economic growth will also increase the affordability of any institutional mechanisms or interventions that are necessary to manage the resources. Also, any necessary institutional changes are often most realistic when seen over a time period of multiple generations, during which attitudes and awareness have a chance to change meaningfully.

A System of Eight Networks

The Vision calls for an extensive national system of eight networks comprised of four core priority networks connected to the mainland, two core priority networks in Zanzibar, a core priority area around Latham Island, and an additional managed network that includes all offshore areas out to the limit of the Exclusive Economic Zone (EEZ). Each network itself contains a number of differently managed areas, either through national recognition such as a formally gazetted Marine Protected Area (MPA), through local designation of a communally managed area, or through lightly regulated areas overseen by

Figure 1.1   Map of Priority Areas for MPA and MMA Networks

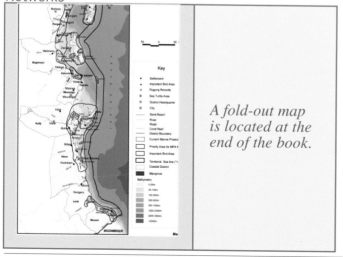

A fold-out map is located at the end of the book.

other authorities. The role of the national system is to describe and provide effective mechanisms for coordinating, supporting, and financing the various networks.

In this book, we define the term "network" to mean a grouping of MPAs and/or marine management areas (MMAs) that are linked, either physically through the movement of organisms and/or water flow, or through common management institutions and personnel. We use the term "system" to describe one or more networks that are set up under a strategically planned, and harmoniously operated, multi-institutional framework. A system recognizes the connectivity of different coastal and marine habitats and has a dual nature: it connects physical sites deemed ecologically critical (ecological networks), and links people and institutions to make effective conservation possible (human networks).

The system design would eventually see some form of protection for the seven near shore core priority networks of 40 percent of the territorial seas within the jurisdiction of Tanzania and Zanzibar. The core networks cover a sub-tidal area of approximately 14 500 km^2; these areas are simply indicative of the general extent of the networks. By contrast, the estimated total coverage of sub-tidal waters by MPAs is currently 1 380 km^2 (this figure includes the closed reefs within the Tanga collaborative fishery management areas). The current protection is equivalent to less than 4 percent of the territorial seas.

Figure 1.1 shows specific areas delineated. The boundaries of these areas are illustrative and themselves somewhat flexible as the system takes shape over the coming decades. To complement these core priority networks, the 200 000 km^2 EEZ (which includes the territorial seas) would possibly be managed under the oversight of the Deep Sea Fishing Authority.

The eight elements of the system include globally and regionally important seascapes within the EAME, and transboundary areas contiguous with those in Kenya and Mozambique.

Figure 1.2 Map of Tanzania's territorial waters

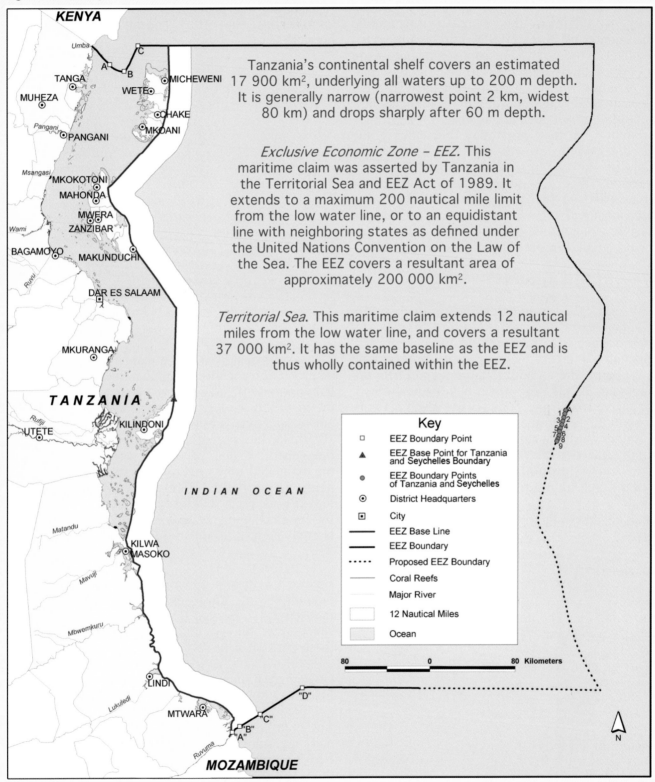

Tanzania's continental shelf covers an estimated 17 900 km², underlying all waters up to 200 m depth. It is generally narrow (narrowest point 2 km, widest 80 km) and drops sharply after 60 m depth.

Exclusive Economic Zone – EEZ. This maritime claim was asserted by Tanzania in the Territorial Sea and EEZ Act of 1989. It extends to a maximum 200 nautical mile limit from the low water line, or to an equidistant line with neighboring states as defined under the United Nations Convention on the Law of the Sea. The EEZ covers a resultant area of approximately 200 000 km².

Territorial Sea. This maritime claim extends 12 nautical miles from the low water line, and covers a resultant 37 000 km². It has the same baseline as the EEZ and is thus wholly contained within the EEZ.

Key

□	EEZ Boundary Point
▲	EEZ Base Point for Tanzania and Seychelles Boundary
●	EEZ Boundary Points of Tanzania and Seychelles
⊙	District Headquarters
⊡	City
——	EEZ Base Line
▬▬	EEZ Boundary
····	Proposed EEZ Boundary
——	Coral Reefs
——	Major River
☐	12 Nautical Miles
▨	Ocean

80   0   80 Kilometers

Core Priority Network 1 – Tanga Region. This includes the districts of Muheza and Pangani, and the Tanga municipality; it includes a total marine area of ~1 600 km^2 as part of a transboundary area with Kenya. The region already has a network of collaborative fishery management areas with closed reefs.

Core Priority Network 2 – Pemba Island. The area (~1 500 km^2 marine) is one of the Zanzibar islands and currently consists of one MPA (Misali) with plans of establishment of Pemba Channel Conservation Area, Wanbaa Makoongwe Conservation area, and extension of the Ngezi Forest Reserve. A number of high quality sites exist within this area, including the Matumbini reef complex, Mtangani reefs, Muongoni Bay, and Ras Kiuyu.

Core Priority Network 3 – Unguja Island. The term Zanzibar is most commonly used in relation to this single island. Officially the island is known as Unguja, while the term Zanzibar refers to the administrative state which includes both this island and Pemba. Within this area (~2 300 km^2 marine), MPAs have been established at Menai Bay, Chumbe, Mnemba, and Jozani-Chwaka Bay; additional MPAs have been recommended at Tumbatu Mwarunga and Nyange reefs and for the islands off Stone Town.

Core Priority Network 4 – Dar es Salaam-Bagamoyo. Within this area (~1 200 km^2 marine) Bagamoyo is considered as subregionally important; pressures from the agglomeration of Dar es Salaam place these nearshore ecosystems under significant threat. Bagamoyo is also important from a cultural heritage perspective and is a potential World Heritage Site.

Core Priority Network 5 – Rufiji-Mafia-Kilwa-Songo Songo complex. The area (~6 700 km^2 marine) is a globally important seascape; potential exists for World Heritage designation for parts of the area, and part of the Rufiji Delta has been proposed as a Ramsar site.

Core Priority Network 6 – Mtwara/Lindi Districts. The area (~1 000 km^2 marine) includes the Mnazi Bay-Ruvuma Estuary Marine Park (MB-REMP), and has significant transboundary importance and potential for World Heritage designation.

Core Priority Network 7 – Latham Island. While a relatively small area (~170 km^2 marine), the small fossil coral oceanic island of less than 3 ha is of critical importance for its masked booby colony, and is also an important breeding site for other seabirds such as sooty terns, brown noddies, swift terns, and black-naped terns. In brief, it is considered the most important seabird island off the coast of East Africa.

Managed Network 8 – EEZ. The area out to the limits of the EEZ (Figure 1.2) is integrated within the system. The total marine area of about 200 000 km^2 overlaps with the marine areas of the above networks, implying co-management of these areas for different resource uses. The area beyond the continental shelf is under the influence of the East African Coastal Current with periodic exchanges of deep water masses. This area is normally fished by foreign vessels.

The "system of networks" concept is based on four interdependent pillars that are the primary focus of this book. These four pillars include:

- **Ecological Protection.** The system is intended to reflect the following ecological characteristics: representativeness, comprehensiveness, adequacy, connectivity and resilience. In achieving this, the system must be adequate in its scale, while reflecting a diversity in its management regimes that captures a precautionary approach and promotes flexibility and adaptation.

- **Poverty Alleviation.** Tanzania is by all accounts a poor country (Table 1.1) and coastal areas are among the poorest regions; on average, 85 percent of the coastal population survive on less than a dollar per person per day. Alternative income generating activities and greater participation through adaptive co-management can improve local livelihoods and reduce the vulnerability of these populations to external shocks.

- **Financial Sustainability.** An overriding concern at both the network and system level is to provide financially sustainable mechanisms that ensure longevity of the resource base. Cost effectiveness and revenue generation are core principles in such sustainability; some experience with this

Photo Dean Housden

Ecological Protection

marine protected area – IUCN definition	Any area of inter-tidal or sub-tidal terrain, together with its overlying water and associated flora, fauna, historical and cultural features, which has been reserved by law or other effective means to protect part or all of the enclosed environment.

The Tanzanian coastline runs approximately north-south and is dominated by three large offshore islands: those of Pemba, Unguja, and Mafia. Among the countries of eastern Africa, Tanzania has the greatest reef area (3 580 km^2). There are fringing and patch reefs along much of the mainland coast and the offshore islands.

Misali Island, just west of Pemba, has some of the country's highest historically recorded coral cover, and high species diversity. Chumbe and Mnemba islands off Zanzibar similarly have diverse and well-protected reefs. Mafia Island has extensive reefs, particularly in the south, many of which remain in good condition. Likewise there are many reefs around the Songo Songo Archipelago in good condition, especially those furthest from the mainland.

There are mangrove forests in most river mouths and sea grass ecosystems are widespread, particularly in the shallow waters around the Mafia and Songo Songo archipelagos. The Rufiji delta supports the largest single mangrove forest in eastern Africa, covering 53 000 ha. Mangroves and shallow coral reefs represent highly diverse and productive systems, which provide important resources for poor people living on the coast.

Protecting these resources meaningfully is a considerable challenge. To guide this challenge, ecological criteria are identified that can assist in designing local networks or larger systems. These are:

is already evident in the URT. In addition, the system calls for revenue sharing mechanisms among stakeholders as well as among areas and networks; this intends to provide equitable rent sharing and a safety net to reduce vulnerability.

● **Institutional Robustness.** The current legislative and institutional setup is relatively comprehensive. But it lacks capacity for implementation, and some issues and gaps remain. The most pressing issue is the extent to which harmonization of instruments and legislation is necessary; we argue that such harmonization is not necessarily a high priority except as it pertains to harmonization of objectives. Key gaps in existing structures relate to the role of traditional use rights, enforcement, and the legal basis for zonation. Many of these gaps can again be addressed most effectively through using adaptive co-management methods that reduce legal uncertainties. A current challenge is to build appropriate institutional models to handle transboundary conservation efforts with neighboring Kenya and Mozambique.

Representativeness. This ensures that all types of biodiversity (both species and habitats) receive protection.

Comprehensiveness. This recognizes the full range of species and ecosystems to be included.

Adequacy. This ensures that the individual components are of sufficient size and appropriate spatial distribution to ensure the ecological viability and integrity of populations and species. In reality, the total amount of ocean gazetted as MPA is less important than whether appropriate amounts of each effectively managed habitat type are included (i.e., whether the network is representative).

Connectivity. This recognizes the linkages between individual components. Connectivity among MPAs, and between MPAs and other areas, is very important given the reproductive characteristics of marine organisms and the physical characteristics of the marine environment.

Resilience. This ensures that the network can survive natural catastrophes and major impacts, by replicating sites that have particularly vulnerable species and ecosystems (e.g., coral reefs).

These criteria translate to some principles of selection and management that include: (i) adequate scale; (ii) precautionary management; and, (iii) adaptive structures. Duplication and redundancy of some types of areas is thus inevitable and desirable, and the use of different management regimes is also required.

How good is the current system? Although it is often stated that protected areas have been created in the past on an *ad hoc* basis, there is in fact a good correspondence between the existing MPAs and the core priority areas for biodiversity conservation in URT. The current system of MPAs (Table 1.2) is thus a good start towards fulfilling these criteria. Only one MPA (Dar es Salaam Marine Reserve System) does not fall in a seascape, but this was established largely for tourism and recreation, rather than biodiversity protection, as it is adjacent to a major urban development. This does not mean that there are enough MPAs, or that they are large enough to ensure adequate representation, but it does indicate that existing MPAs form a sound baseline for the development of a representative system.

Many alternatives are available as starting points for designing systems. Networks can be based on individual species, or on specific ecosystems. But such approaches would not generally meet the diverse requirements of the country's coastal populations. Throughout east Africa (including the URT) there has, for example, been an overemphasis on coral reefs in MPA design, while mangroves and wetlands are largely under-represented. An optimal approach is therefore that reflected in the proposed System of Networks comprising the seven core priority areas and the EEZ.

Within Blueprint 2050, the sub-tidal area of about 14 500 km^2 falling within the near shore core priority networks would include virtually all of the country's coral reefs, mangroves, coastal wetlands, and important bird areas. Moreover, 40 percent of the territorial seas and about 80 percent of the continental shelf would fall under some form of protection or management important to critical species throughout the EEZ.

Table 1.1 Country information: Tanzania

Population (2002)	35.2 million
Life expectancy at birth (2002)	43
Under-5 mortality rate (2002)	165 per 1000
Gross national income (2002)	US$290/capita
Rural population below the poverty line (2000-2001)	38.7 percent
Ranking on the Human Development Index (2002)	162 (out of 177)

Sources: 2004 World Development Report, World Bank, 2004; 2004 Human Development Report, UNDP, 2004.

Poverty Alleviation

Tanzania has made significant progress in liberalizing its economy and stabilizing its macroeconomic environment. Inflation has been brought under control and economic growth averaged about 4 percent during the last five years. Despite these achievements, poverty levels have remained high—even though the country is endowed with a rich natural resource base, has good geographical access to international markets, and has maintained a politically stable environment. Poverty is especially widespread in rural areas where some 87 percent of the population is considered poor. The levels of poverty, and vulnerability, are highest in the coastal regions (especially in the Pwani and Lindi regions).

The coastal areas of Tanzania are of critical importance for the development of the country. The five coastal regions of mainland Tanzania contribute about one third of the national GDP. Coastal areas are becoming increasingly important in promoting economic growth in Tanzania—some 75 percent of the country's industries are located on the coast. The potential for increasing the share of foreign exchange earnings from sustainable development of the coastal tourism industry in both mainland Tanzania and Zanzibar is very significant. Bio-prospecting and research to identify other potential values of sponges, soft corals, tunicates, and different sea-weeds, are growing industries just beginning exploratory research along the Eastern African coast.

Coastal resources have come under increasing pressures over the past three decades, which has led to a significant decline in the natural resource base. Consequently, the livelihoods of coastal communities are under increasing threat and vulnerability. This represents a risk not only for the people that directly depend on these resources for food and income, but also for the industries that generate significant revenues from these resources for the nation. A System of Networks potentially addresses such issues. But if the system does not benefit coastal populations, increased degradation and a decrease in the services provided by the existing coastal ecosystems may ultimately occur, leading to marginalized livelihoods and greater poverty. Thus, there is a need for any managed areas (formal MPAs as well as community managed areas) to contribute to the economic development of coastal areas by integrating local economic development with sustainable natural resource management.

To achieve this, two key elements are required. First, *we need adequate levels of alternative income generating activities* (AIGAs) that promote sustainable resource use or, minimally, do not interfere with it. Such AIGAs must also try to promote savings and reinvestment in the natural resource base, habits that are not as evident in coastal communities as they are further inland. Second, we require meaningful decision-making vested in those immediately affected by resource use impacts. For this, *we advocate models of adaptive co-management* (ACM) that involve multiple stakeholders, take advantage of (and rely on) local traditions and conditions, and use flexible methods of management that respond to learning opportunities.

Tanzania already has some experience using AIGAs within ACM systems and they warrant further testing and replication elsewhere. The Tanga Coastal Zone Conservation and Development Program, initiated in 1994 in response to declining fish resources, is acknowledged world wide as a practical example of the application of effective methods for highly decentralized community-based coastal management; local initiatives have piloted mariculture and seaweed farming. In Zanzibar, the Misali Island and Menai Bay Conservation Projects involve co-management at three levels—local, district

Table 1.2 Protected and managed marine areas in the URT

As of mid-2004, mainland Tanzania and Zanzibar include 1 380 km² of Marine Protected Areas (MPAs) and Marine Management Areas (MMAs) within their territorial seas. Various Integrated Coastal Management initiatives or proposed extensions to terrestrial parks provide opportunities for increasing this amount.

	Date Established*	Sub-tidal Area (km²)
MAINLAND TANZANIA (870 km²)		
Dar es Salaam Marine Reserves System – comprises 4 islands, designated as Marine Reserves in 1975, and placed under the mandate of MPRU in 1998	1975	26.0
Maziwe Island Marine Reserve	1981	2.6
Mafia Island Marine Park (total = 822 km²) – multiple use marine park with zoning	1995	615.0
Tanga collaborative fishery management areas (~1603 km², of which 29 km² is no-take) – covers coastal areas of Muheza, Tanga and Pangani districts; set up as joint initiatives between local communities and districts; area includes closed reefs and Maziwe Island Marine Reserve	1996-2000	26.4
Mnazi Bay-Ruvuma Estuary Marine Park (total area = 650 km²)	2000	200.0
Saadani National Park: a new protected area, up-grading the previous Game Reserve, and potentially extending protection into the sea	2004	
Kinondoni Integrated Coastal Area Management Program	2000	
Rufiji Environmental Management Program – a large program covering the entire delta, but with a coastal component	1998	
ZANZIBAR (510 km²)		
Chumbe Island Coral Sanctuary (all no-take) – management delegated to a private company	1994	0.3
Menai Bay Conservation Area – a community-managed MPA	1997	470.0
Misali Island Marine Conservation Area (total area 23 km² includes terrestrial; no-take = 1.4 km²) – an NGO and community-managed MPA	1998	21.6
Mnemba Island Marine Conservation Area** (no-take zone) – as part of MIMCA, a privately managed MPA on Mnemba Island is supported through Conservation Corporation Africa	2002	0.15
Kiwengwa Controlled Area – established in 2000 but never managed	2000	17.5
Ngezi Forest Reserve (14.4 km²) – proposed for re-designation as a Nature Reserve; includes mangroves and beach	1959	
Jozani National Park – a pilot ICM site and protected forest area, Zanzibar's first national park	2004	

*The Date Established normally shows the date that the sub-tidal area was included; some sites that include land were designated as terrestrial protected areas earlier. For Saadani National Park, which was established as a Game Reserve in 1964, no sub-tidal area has yet been declared. Dates for ICM programs in Kinondoni and Rufiji are the start date of the programs.

**Mnemba Island Marine Conservation Area beyond the no-take zone now includes the Kiwengwa Controlled Area and Chwaka Bay. It extends from Nungwi (north of Unguja) to Chwaka Bay, through Mnemba, Kiwengwa, Marumbi, Charawe, Michamvi and Ukongoroni villages, and is co-managed by community and government.

The Coelacanth – *A Lost Species Rediscovered.*

The coelacanth is a fish that was known only through 300 million year old fossil records and was thought to have been extinct for 80 million years. Since its rediscovery in 1938 in S Africa, individual specimens have been caught from time to time, and its abundance and range may be more widespread than previously assumed.

In late 2003 a coelacanth was caught off southern Tanzania at Songa Mnara Island, followed by a catch off Moheli in the Comoros and then just a day later, another in Hahaya, north of Grand Comoro.

The finds extend the known habitat range of this fish. Coelacanths have never been found at Moheli and the only previous capture off Tanzania was an unconfirmed one at Mafia Island.

The fish found in Tanzania was caught by a local fishermen in a net in just 100 m depth of water. The fish was recognized amongst the many on the island left out to dry in the sun. The fish had already been cut with all its insides thrown away. Mr Rumisha, manager of the Marine Parks and Reserves Unit Tanzania, and colleague Prof Bwathondi later positively identified the fish and worked around the clock to try and preserve the specimen. The fish was 132 cm and without its insides weighed 22 kg.

Photographs by courtesy of the African Coelacanth Ecosystem Programme, South African Institute for Aquatic Biodiversity (SAIAB)

and national – and are instrumental in protecting and managing the access rights of almost 2000 and 1800 fishermen respectively while providing income for local development and income earning initiatives. Innovative tourism-based models – such as the Chumbe Island Coral Park Ltd – have also provided a rich experience by involving the private sector as a key partner in generating employment and managing public resources. AIGAs thus can contribute meaningfully to reducing pressures on the resource base, and alleviating poverty.

What is perhaps least clear are the precise conditions under which formal MPAs can contribute to poverty alleviation. Background studies in 24 coastal villages in Tanzania suggest that there is little difference in the poverty rates of fishing households in villages that are in or near MPAs, compared to those outside of MPAs. The establishment of MPAs does, however, appear to have a significant impact on poverty rates

among those households that can benefit from the alternative employment opportunities generated; employment rates typically double under the presence of an MPA, across all income levels. This again suggests the need for a flexible, adaptive environment that permits adjustments to be made to management models as more is learned.

Blueprint 2050 has a substantial challenge to address. The coastal population – at that time – will approach 20 million people. Currently some 87 percent of the coastal rural population lives in poverty, well above the national rural average (50 percent) and far above the Millennium Development Goals (MDG) for sub-Saharan Africa, which set a 2015 target of 24 percent. A System of Networks can contribute positively to alleviating poverty. A dollar a day, which is the notional poverty line in the MDG for sub-Saharan Africa, has already been achieved at some of the country's managed areas. Activities at

Misali Island – Local Conditions Influence Management Opportunities.

Misali is a small (0.9 km²) forested island of coral rag surrounded by a ring of coral, located 10 km west of Pemba Island. No one lives on Misali permanently, but it provides a campground for fishermen who stay there for shorter periods of time. Over 1500 fishermen, living in some 30 villages around Pemba, are active in the Misali waters. It is estimated that about 11 000 people directly depend on Misali for food and income.

Misali Island is highly respected by the surrounding communities, many of whom believe that the island has religious significance and spiritual characteristics. There is a common belief that one of the Prophets (Nabii Hadhir AS) once came to Misali, where he asked for a prayer mat. When he found out that there was no mat, he asserted that "the island is like a prayer mat (kisiwa cha mithali ya msala) because it points exactly towards the Alkaaba in Mecca." He prayed and then disappeared. According to this myth, this is how the island got its name, Misali, which in Kiswahili means mithali. There are also ancestor healing/divination sites on the island and there are taboos related to specific activities (e.g., women are not allowed to sleep on the island). All these traditions have made it easier to combine traditional, religious and

Mafia Island Marine Park (MIMP) – ranging from handicrafts to seaweed farming to beekeeping – have generated incomes approaching US$10 a day to participating members, much of which is then spent locally to generate further economic benefits. Poverty eradication is possible. It requires expanding current lessons to the entire coastal area and finding models that permit such an expansion. This may not be achievable in a typical five year project timeframe, but it is a realistic goal within the next two to three generations.

Financial Sustainability

Some of the poverty reduction that has occurred has been at significant external expense. Traditional aid projects often leave behind a legacy of expensive equipment with little hope of covering operational costs. A review of some such projects shows that own-revenue generation at marine parks is typically covering at best one half of operating costs. At the Menai Bay Conservation Area in 2002, for example, annual tourism receipts were about Tsh40 million while operating costs for the structures put in place approach Tsh90 million. A financially sustainable protected area, network, or system must somehow address this issue.

It is important to distinguish between financial sustainability and economic sustainability. The two are similar, but not identical. In the case of economic sustainability, welfare improvements through poverty reduction, increased incomes, or increased employment exceed any costs associated with such improvements. In short, benefits exceed costs. There is ample evidence in Tanzania and elsewhere that the benefit:cost ratio of sustainable resource management in coastal areas far exceeds unity. But many of the benefits are not readily captured (such as traditional uses of marine products by local

Photo Dear Housden

where MPAs and management areas are set up and managed by a number of different agencies. In URT, several government agencies are involved. The lead agencies include the Marine Parks and Reserves Unit (MPRU) and the Tanzania National Parks Authority (TANAPA) on the mainland, and the Department of Fisheries and the Department of Commercial Crops, Fruits and Forestry (DCCFF) on Zanzibar; local government, local communities and the private sector are also key partners. Harmonization does not mean that all the components of the network will be managed or overseen by a single authority. Blueprint 2050 advocates a continuation of the full range of management approaches, along with the introduction of a coordinating mechanism to provide guidance and to ensure sharing of lessons learned and expertise.

Cost reductions are most evident where private sector partners have been engaged to assist in management. For example, the Chumbe Island initiative has been successful at keeping costs down while still spending adequately on education, conservation, and MPA staff. Conservation related expenditures at Chumbe Island are 20 percent of the total cost base, and the private sector enterprise is financially sustainable so long as it maintains occupancy rates in the 30-50 percent range.

Revenue and rent collection is a serious concern. Evidence suggests that in many cases resources are being mismanaged because "prices are not right," meaning that too little is being charged for the product or the service. While in some places tourists are paying premium prices for access to marine areas, in others the fee is negligible for a similar experience. Tourists typically pay of the order of US$25-50 daily to marine park authorities elsewhere in the world as a trip surcharge, whereas under new regulations in Mnemba Island Marine Conservation Area, they had been paying only US$1 a trip to a community fund; this was increased to US$3 as of June 2004. Under-pricing is also common with fisheries resources; the regulatory structure for deep sea fishing captures less than 5 percent of the landed value of the resource; this is entirely inadequate to monitor and regulate a fishery that covers 200 000 km^2 of seas. Numerous mechanisms exist for improving this situation, and it is expected that all will be used where appropriate.

communities) or they accrue to stakeholders who themselves are not bearing any of the costs (such as foreign fishing fleets). Financial sustainability, by contrast, considers more closely the cash that accrues and is available to meet resource management costs. In simplest terms, financial sustainability occurs when the available revenues cover the management cost plus an additional precautionary margin to meet unforeseen circumstances (such as normal fluctuations in resource availability, or impacts of natural or man-made disasters). In this book, our focus on financial sustainability has four elements: (i) cost effectiveness through using the most efficient means to achieve a given end; (ii) revenue collection, through targeting and retaining the highest value resources in a manner that still permits their sustainable use; (iii) equitable revenue sharing through using instruments and models that reinforce local management efforts; and, (iv) precautionary instruments to provide safety nets that reduce the vulnerability of individual networks, subsystems and managed areas.

Blueprint 2050 addresses all of these elements and, again, can draw on preliminary experience within Tanzania. A major advantage of a system of networks is that the benefits and costs of management – in terms of financing, technical input and staff capacity – can be spread across sites. Some harmonization of management approaches, to reflect national policy, will also be simpler. This is particularly important

Even if costs are kept down and revenues are substantial, management efforts may be unsuccessful if inadequate or unfair revenue sharing schemes prevail. An internal review of the Menai Bay project cited lack of clear revenue sharing mechanisms as a major constraint to financial sustainability. Arbitrary and unclear taxation schemes are frequently cited by the private sector as constraints to investment. Local development initiatives often come to a grinding halt if tourism numbers suddenly drop because of external factors; this occurred after the 2003 travel advisories in the wake of terrorist threats in East Africa. Blueprint 2050 calls for a two-pronged approach to revenue sharing. At the local level, adaptive co-management processes should define and entrench revenue sharing arrangements with clarity and certainty; such arrangements should be adequate to provide local incentives for proper resource management, as well as sustainable financing for expected costs. At a higher level (local network and system level) a pooled precautionary funding mechanism is advocated that collects revenues from multiple sources, while redistributing those funds for priority areas with low own-revenue generation, or providing a buffer for any area during times of urgency.

Under Blueprint 2050, each MPA or MMA would use best available mechanisms to reduce costs and maximize revenues locally, sharing these burdens and benefits according to protocols established through co-management agreements. Those areas that generate routine surpluses pay partially into a common funding pool – we call this a Marine Legacy Fund. Those areas of national priority that require subsidy can draw from this funding pool. The revolving nature of the Marine Legacy Fund is intended to provide adequate buffer for periodic shocks (revenue shortfalls or emergency expenditures), while also taking advantage of replenishment through other sources, such as routine budget allocations, revenue shares from offshore fishery rents, selected fines and levies, and potential external assistance or budget support. We estimate the minimum capital of such a Marine Legacy Fund to be of the order of US$50 million to provide an adequate buffer for the core elements of the system, although it could conceivably fluctuate from between US$25 and US$100 million depending on year to year circumstances.

Institutional Robustness

Mainland Tanzania and Zanzibar are autonomous for environmental issues, including wildlife and fisheries. Because of their experience with protected areas, they both have considerable legislation and institutions to handle the management of such resources. Any MPA and other MMA within the territorial seas is thus not a Union issue, although initiatives in the wider EEZ would be considered a Union issue. Institutional and legal mechanisms for managing any system are thus of critical importance.

As a starting point, we note that there are few gaps in the overall institutional and legal structure. A key constraint remains lack of institutional ability to enforce some of the mandates, and for this reason there is considerable enthusiasm for measures and models that permit decentralization of decision-making and enforcement closer to the resource base. Private sector models, and those involving active community participation represent such structures.

Outstanding issues within the context of Blueprint 2050 relate to harmonization of policies, specific issues respecting decentralization of effort, and general institutional modalities for the EEZ and internationally important protected areas.

Harmonization can be regarded from two perspectives: harmonization of objectives; and harmonization of ways and means. At present, the ways and means of protected area management differ considerably between mainland Tanzania and Zanzibar. But the overall objectives are compatible. This suggests to us that different models can co-exist and be used to a common purpose. In effect, this "difference of means – similarity of purpose," can also be applied at a lower level – to individual networks, to individual MPAs or MMAs, or to neighboring managed areas. Diversity of methods and flexibility in model design is an important characteristic of the system.

To implement effective decentralized management, however, some legislative gaps need to be addressed. First, existing legislation provides inadequate recognition and attention to traditional use rights; co-managed local areas will require strengthening

Harmonized Objectives, Different Means – the Case of Mainland Tanzania and Zanzibar.

For **mainland Tanzania**, *the purpose of an MPA as defined under the Marine Parks and Reserves Act is to:*

- *Protect and restore marine and coastal biodiversity and ecosystem resources.*
- *Stimulate rational development of under-utilized resources.*
- *Manage marine and coastal areas to promote sustainability of existing resource use and recovery of over-exploited/damaged areas and resources.*
- *Ensure involvement and benefit sharing of local communities.*
- *Promote education and information dissemination.*
- *Facilitate research and monitoring.*

MPAs may incorporate additional purposes as required; for example, Mafia Island Marine Park has two further purposes: conservation of historic monuments and cultural resources; and facilitation of ecotourism development.

For **Zanzibar**, *the Environment Act states the purpose of the protected area system as:*

- *Preservation.*
- *Sustainable utilization by those living in or near the protected area.*
- *Propagation of genetic resources for conservation in other areas.*
- *Education.*
- *Management of biological diversity.*
- *Scientific research.*
- *Environmentally sound tourism and recreation.*

Also, each protected area has stated management objectives in its management plan or legislation.

of legislation to make arrangements clear and protect traditional interests. Second, enforcement authority and responsibility in a decentralized context often lacks clarity in existing institutional and legal frameworks. Finally, actual authority for zonation in decentralized models is ill-defined. This will naturally require more input from district and local authorities than has heretofore been the case. One potential mechanism for addressing all of these issues would be through the entrenchment of near shore rights through – for example – a 3 km or 5 km management zone in which districts and the communities within them have explicit and specific rights and obligations. We call this zone a "Community Territorial Sea." Any near shore management zone within the Territorial Seas would, of course, remain under shared jurisdiction with national authorities. Such a co-management model has been applied in

other countries with some success and would be an appropriate starting point for URT in helping clarify many management issues.

A significant institutional challenge involves dealing with far offshore resources and those with potentially jointly managed jurisdictions with other sovereign governments. In the case of the EEZ and fisheries management, the most advanced initiative involves the establishment of the Deep Sea Fishing Authority; this Authority would have a mandate to manage resources to the limits of Tanzania's claimed 200 nm limit. Many of the responsibilities of this body, or any body that would have a similar function, remain to be established and negotiated within the overall context of Union issues. Entrenching this function is a current priority of government and could also be an important institutional link in the Blueprint 2050 system.

Tanzania's Global and Regional Initiatives for Marine Protection.

Tanzania is part of significant international initiatives to protect marine resources. The World Heritage Convention – to which URT is a signatory – protects sites that are outstanding examples of the world's cultural and natural heritage. Kilwa (where the ruins have already been designated a cultural World Heritage Site) and the Mnazi Bay/Ruvuma Estuary are included among these sites for their coastal, marine and small island biodiversity attributes. The Kenya/Tanzania transboundary areas near Shimoni-Tanga and Pemba are also among these sites.

The UNESCO Man and the Biosphere Programme is another global network of protected areas, but it is not based on a convention. Biosphere Reserves are designated to encourage a broad range of objectives linking humans and the environment. As with World Heritage Sites, such areas must have some form of protection under national legislation before being accepted for designation as a Biosphere Reserve. The general structure of a Biosphere Reserve is a core protected area with a surrounding larger buffer zone which may be inhabited and exploited under sustainable use regimes. Biosphere Reserves are thus similar in approach to many multiple-use MPAs (e.g., Mafia and Mnazi Bay marine parks), and to MMAs supporting a variety of uses. Consideration is being given to developing a Biosphere Reserve in the Kilwa-Rufiji area.

At the regional level, URT is already a major participant in regional initiatives that are contributing to the development of MPAs and marine management areas at different scales. At the level of the African continent, these include the African Protected Areas Initiative and the newly revised African Convention. At the level of the Western Indian Ocean and Eastern Africa, URT is involved in: (i) programs in the East African Marine Ecoregion; (ii) the UNEP Regional Seas East African Programme; (iii) various programs associated with the Large Marine Ecosystems; (iv) a proposed South West Indian Ocean Fisheries Commission; and (v) a regional component of a project supported by the Global Environment Facility – the Global Coral Reef Targeted Research and Capacity Building for Management Project.

A second institutional challenge relates to the management and funding of transboundary protected areas. For example, as part of the collaborative fishery management planning in Muheza district in the north, discussions are being initiated in Kenya with Kwale district and the Kenya Wildlife Service which manages Kisite Marine Park/Mpunguti Marine Reserve. Also, as part of the development of Mnazi Bay-Ruvuma Estuary Marine Park, discussions are being initiated with northern Mozambique; the focus is on the province of Cabo Delgado where conservation areas are being identified within an Integrated Coastal Management (ICM) initiative.

Next Steps

The Vision elaborated above has a number of key elements. Spatially, it consists of a system based on precautionary design principles that will eventually see the management of some 40 percent of the territorial seas. Institutionally, integrated planning will be necessary in such a context, and the planning must support capacity building that promotes adaptive co-management as well as diversification of alternative income generating activities. Some new concepts may also be operationalized over the coming decades. The Vision calls for establishment of a Marine Legacy Fund to pool financial risks and to create a buffer against uncertainty. The Vision also proposes that a Community Territorial Sea be included within marine zonation plans, with explicit management rights conferred to coastal districts.

Government commitment to sustainable use of the coastal areas is already evident. Serious efforts are being pursued to advance legislation and to implement projects that will improve coastal management. Obviously, the next step is to engage in a broader dialogue that permits discussion of this Vision, and adoption of it after appropriate modification within the context of global, regional, national and local realities.

But the greatest challenges will be within mainland Tanzania and Zanzibar themselves. For Blueprint 2050 to be realized, political commitment to two complementary elements is required: local awareness building; and, the collection and management of scientific information. These two elements are extremely different in character and scope, but in a sense show the breadth of commitment that is necessary for this Vision to be realized.

Local awareness building is important for short-term success and acceptance, and requires engagement of every possible stakeholder in the planning process. Surveys conducted for this book showed that – of those individuals unhappy with having marine parks or other managed areas in their proximity – 37 percent of those cited "restriction of access to resources" as their major complaint. Monitoring such perceptions is important and, if this viewpoint persists, it is unlikely that any comprehensive proposal for marine management will be acceptable. In some instances the viewpoint is valid, and in those cases local management regimes need to be altered. In other instances, the viewpoints are not substantiated by actual evidence, and in such cases sensitization may be necessary. In yet other instances, the viewpoints are simply prejudged positions that support a different agenda, and are likely unalterable; in these cases, promotion of local co-management and governance structures can improve overall transparency and, eventually, offset such influences.

A commitment to sound scientific knowledge management is also critical to long-term management in any adaptive structure, and monitoring efforts will be necessary at all levels to provide adequate information. The current information base for making decisions on protected area designation and management is of mixed quality and coverage. There are no coordinating institutions, or managed data collection efforts, that cover all potentially affected areas. Development of a national biogeographical classification could

contribute significantly to this gap. Also, institutional arrangements for information management are required; URT currently has inadequate capacity for effective information management of this nature, but a number of institutions now have the basic equipment and skills.

Finally, it must be recognized that in some cases it may be quite impossible to implement or sustainably manage local MPAs, community fishing areas, or more complex models. In a learning environment such places will be released so as not to cause a drain on other parts of the system. Blueprint 2050 envisions a flexible and diverse system: it can and should expand from its current sound base; but it might in due course also contract as circumstances change.

Blueprint 2050 is thus as much a process as it is a template. The process will rely heavily on knowledge management and generation of the best available information for decision-making. If we acknowledge that we are not designing the system but, rather, are partners in its evolution, then the emergence of a complex system that works, from simple systems that work, will be inevitable.

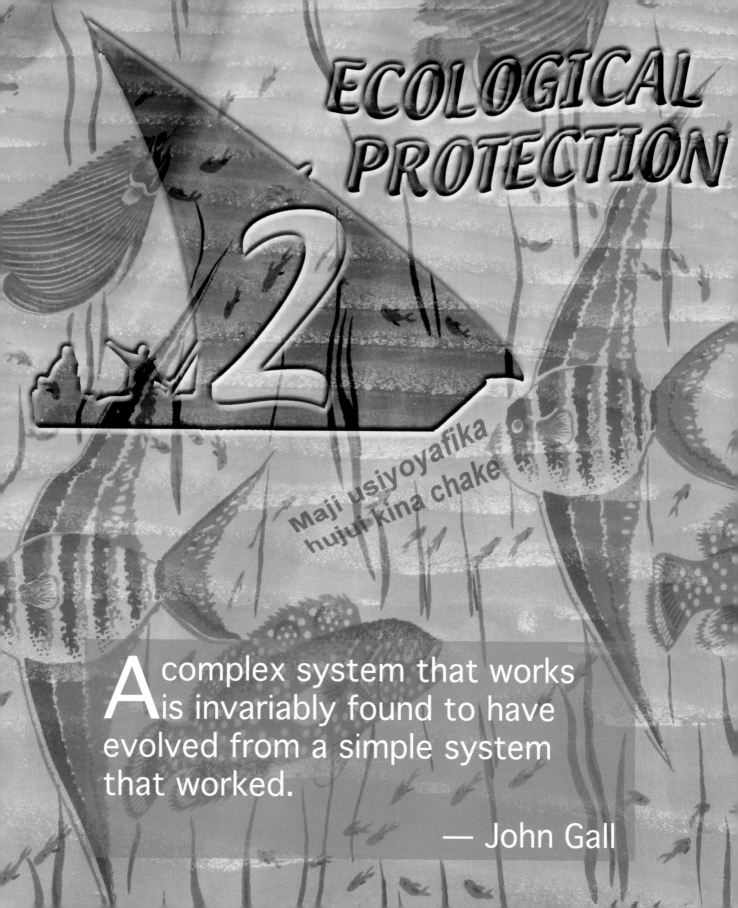

ECOLOGICAL PROTECTION

2

Maji usiyoyafika
hujui kina chake

A complex system that works
is invariably found to have
evolved from a simple system
that worked.

— John Gall

Introduction

URT has the opportunity to take a bold and innovative approach to hosting a system of marine protected areas (MPAs) and marine management areas (MMAs). This book calls for the development of networks of marine management areas, that would be coordinated to form a national system. The system is characterized by a handful of core priority networks; within these networks a diversity of management models can be applied. The core networks provisionally identified include four along the mainland coast (Tanga Region, Dar es Salaam-Bagamoyo, Rufiji-Mafia-Kilwa-Songo Songo complex, and Mtwara/Lindi districts), two comprising the marine areas of the Zanzibar islands (Pemba, Unguja), and one oceanic island (Latham Island). In addition, the EEZ can be considered as an eighth network which is to be sustainably managed.

Establishing such a mixed system, with subregional networks, would not entail the immediate development of many new MPAs other than those recently proposed, but it would require that MPAs be systematically linked to each other. For each site, effective protection requires coordination of efforts at the national, district, and local level, as well as a coming together of many different disciplines.

In this chapter, we look at the ecological issues and concepts surrounding the evolution of this system and the selection of priority sites. In so doing, we commence with a review of some key concepts, then take a snapshot of today's ecological conditions in mainland Tanzania's and Zanzibar's coastal areas. We then look at the goals of what such a system should consider, showing the implications that such goals have on system scale, precautionary design, and adaptive management. Before describing in greater detail the approach advocated here, we consider some alternative approaches to designing a system. As an endpoint, we anticipate that over the following decades – if such a bold approach is taken – Tanzania would see upwards of 40 percent protection of its territorial seas (compared to about 4 percent today), and comprehensive management of all fisheries and other resources in the EEZ.

Photo Indu Hewawasam

The quote at this chapter-head stresses that systems tend to evolve rather than be outright designed. We embrace this as well, advocating and expecting that any system that does serve to promote protection and sustainable use will, by necessity, be adaptive. Fundamentally, the system will be comprised of ecological subsystems and human subsystems. Ecological subsystems – be they mangroves, coral reefs, sea grasses, river estuaries – will all adapt to external stresses. Sea levels may rise, floods may become more pronounced, rains may fail; each of these stresses in turn elicits an adaptation in the ecosystem. Similarly, people adapt. If fisheries fail, people will turn to other forms of nutrition. If opportunities arise in the city, people will migrate from the rural areas. In the wake of a sudden construction boom, people will start mining sand from previously pristine beaches. Any system that comprises ecosystems and humans is, by definition, adaptive. The most common failure in systems design comes from ignoring this fact: systems – even those forming collectives of protected or managed areas – must have in-built mechanisms and processes that promote learning and flexibility.

Exploring some Concepts – An Ecologist Speaks

Many of the ecological terms and definitions we will use throughout this book are in common use in the literature. Even so, some of these definitions can have multiple meanings, and misunderstandings often arise because of ill-defined terms. As a starting point, therefore, we ask our resident ecologist to elaborate.

This book addresses Marine Protected Areas (MPAs), but also other types of areas. Who in fact defines what an MPA is?

Any country can use whatever definition it prefers, but there is some benefit to having a common understanding of what an MPA is. The most widely used definition of an MPA is that of the International Union for the Conservation of Nature (IUCN). The IUCN is more officially known as the "World Conservation Union" and is the organization that maintains the lists of threatened and endangered species.

What is IUCN's definition of an MPA?

The IUCN defines an MPA as "Any area of inter-tidal or sub-tidal terrain, together with its overlying water and associated flora, fauna, historical and cultural features, which has been reserved by law or other effective means to protect part or all of the enclosed environment." This intentionally broad definition covers all types of marine areas with protection (regardless of their name, such as marine reserve, sanctuary, and marine park) *provided their primary objective is biodiversity protection*. Other managed areas with similar objectives might have "resource management for sustainable development" rather than "biodiversity protection" as a primary objective, and would therefore not be termed "protected areas" by IUCN.

How does Tanzania regard MPAs?

URT is a member of IUCN and in general uses the IUCN approach to protected areas. This book therefore uses the term MPA for sites meeting the IUCN definition, and refers to other managed areas as "marine management areas" (MMAs). MPAs and MMAs in the URT may also include a terrestrial component – such as an island or some coastal area above the high-tide mark.

Where do the ideas of "networks" and "systems" come from, and what is their goal?

The concept of networks and systems of protected areas has had a relatively short history of testing and application but has been much discussed in the scientific literature, for both the terrestrial and marine environments. Other related terms found in the literature include ecological networks, bioregional/ecoregional planning, biological corridors, and the ecosystem approach. All aim to promote planning at the broad level and to develop cross-sectoral partnerships.

Do the two terms mean the same thing?

The terms "system" and "network" are often used interchangeably to describe a group of protected areas spread across a country or region, with defined linkages between them. Neither term yet has a globally accepted definition. But many practitioners perceive differences. IUCN's World Commission on Protected Areas has suggested that a "network" has a mainly geographical and physical sense, and recognizes connectivity between the components, which in some cases may be a physical connection. By contrast, a "system" has a functional sense in that, as well as describing geographical and physical relationships, it implies consistent institutional and managerial arrangements, with coordinated planning. According to such an understanding, "network" is often used when "system" is probably meant.

Blueprint 2050 describes a system of eight networks. What definitions does it use?

It relies strongly on the suggested IUCN understanding. A "network" is a grouping of MPAs and/or marine management areas that are linked physically through the movement of organisms or water flow. A "system" is one or more networks that are set up under a strategically planned, and harmoniously operated, multi-institutional framework. A system recognizes the connectivity of different coastal and marine habitats, and it has a dual nature: it connects physical sites deemed ecologically critical (a system of ecological networks), and links people and institutions in order to make effective conservation and management possible (a system of human networks).

How does such a system of networks promote ecological objectives?

Although there is a trend towards a systems approach to MPA planning in some countries, MPAs have been identified and established in a largely ad hoc and opportunistic manner in most places. Agencies have tended to follow their own mandates without considering the bigger picture beyond their geographical and sectoral boundaries. Recognizing that marine ecosystems, species, and coastal communities are inexorably linked, and that piecemeal efforts to protect the marine environment have been largely unsuccessful, there is an obvious need for strategically developed systems.

Why is it important in Tanzania?

The marine and coastal ecosystems of URT, and the communities that comprise them, are linked to each other through a complex web of ecological and oceanographic processes. The two monsoons have marked effects on the ocean environment of the URT. Winds are a particularly important feature, driving water circulation and affecting wave action, local climate, biological processes and human activities. Equally important is the impact of currents, both large oceanic and tidal currents, and of freshwater inflow. All these processes influence the dispersal of larvae, nutrients, pollutants and other biological and inorganic matter and thus have an important bearing on the design of a system of protected areas.

The various parts of the mainland coast and the offshore islands are also linked by migrating species, such as turtles, fish and marine mammals, that breed or nest in one area and feed in others. Research on the connectivity of ecosystems and species populations in the marine environment is relatively new. Data on migration patterns of turtles and some marine mammals have been available for some time through tagging and observation programs, but techniques have only recently become available for studying adult and larval dispersal. For many species, data are lacking and options for a system must be flexible and able to take into account new information that may become available later.

You also mentioned the connection to human activities. Presumably there is a complementary role whereby connecting people also achieves certain ecosystem management goals?

Yes, the use of marine and coastal resources in human activities is also best thought of at the broad scale, rather than simply at the local level. This is particularly the case for fisheries, tourism, and community livelihoods which are the predominant economic activities that will influence the design of an MPA system in URT. The establishment of marine management areas (particularly zones that are closed to fishing) may affect some sectors of society to the extent that they will need to find employment opportunities elsewhere. A system of MPAs and MMAs can take this into account.

Tourism has been slated for major expansion in URT in the coming decades. Plans for priority areas for tourism development have already been drawn up, and indeed most of the mainland coast is designated as a priority area in the 2002 National Tourism Strategy. MPAs are likely to be a key attraction for tourists, while also playing a role in safeguarding marine biodiversity from any damaging industrial impacts. Tourism development plans must therefore be considered in the development of a system.

Thank you very much. In closing, what would you regard as the most significant challenges in putting together a system of networks of MPAs and other marine managed areas.

There are two related challenges. First, we need an ongoing commitment to improve our scientific understanding of the ecosystems we are trying to manage or protect. Second, we require an adaptive and flexible system that can respond to any new information or new needs; traditional models are often too inflexible. In mainland Tanzania and Zanzibar, we are starting from a rather irregular scientific basis: we know a lot about a few things and very little about a lot of things. In such circumstances, an adaptive approach is even more important.

Point of Departure

General Overview

The URT comprises the mainland coast, three principal islands (Pemba, Unguja, and Mafia), numerous small nearshore islands and islets, and one oceanic island (Latham). The continental shelf is generally narrow ranging from 2 km at its narrowest point, to 80 km at its widest. It covers an area of 17 900 km^2 and drops sharply after 60-200 m depth. Pemba and Latham are separated from the mainland by relatively deep water, 400-500 m and 200-300 m depth respectively. Pemba is believed to be part of the mainland that broke away about 10 million years ago. Unguja and Mafia are limestone islands on the continental shelf and were probably part of a Pleistocene inshore coral reef system which is now separated from the mainland by relatively shallow (30-50 m deep) channels.

Important marine ecosystems in the URT include mangrove forests, estuaries, coral reefs, sea grass beds and inter-tidal flats. Coral reefs are found around much of the coastline of Tanzania, and are most extensive around Tanga, Kilwa, Mtwara, and the islands of Unguja, Pemba, and the Songo Songo archipelago. Mangroves are found in most river mouths, with the Rufiji river delta supporting the largest single mangrove forest in eastern Africa. These ecosystems support a very high diversity of plant and animal species including marine mammals, marine turtles, coastal and sea birds, fish, plankton, sponges, crustaceans, mollusks, echinoderms and a variety of other organisms.

The ecosystems and species play a major role in the health and functioning of the coastal and marine environment, which in turn affects the livelihoods of the people who depend on this environment: an estimated 40 000 artisanal fishermen land about 50 000 tons of fish annually. The potential yield of marine fish from URT's territorial waters is at least 100 000 metric tons; current annual production of marine invertebrates (shrimps, lobsters, crabs, octopus, squids, seashells and sea cucumbers) is about 1 400 metric tons.

However, the coastal and marine environment of URT is facing unprecedented risks and threats from human activities and natural phenomena including:

- Over-exploitation (of, for example, mangroves, sea cucumbers, lobster, shrimps, octopus, shells and corals).

- Destructive fishing methods (fish dynamiting, poisoning, beach seining).

- Industrial and domestic pollution (oil spills, effluents, wastes).

- Potential unregulated tourism development.

- Global climate change.

These impacts are being felt as much in URT as they are elsewhere in the world, with the destruction and loss of critical habitats such as coral reefs and sea grass beds. Landings of many commercially important marine species have declined tremendously, despite an increase in catch effort, resulting in reduced revenue generation opportunities for coastal people and consequent high poverty levels.

Recent research has indicated that marine and coastal ecosystems are less resilient than previously thought. The extinction risk to marine species, once thought to be inexhaustible on account of their presumed large ranges and abundance, is much higher than previously understood. Many species have relatively small distributions and others, such as sharks and large predatory fish, are highly vulnerable to exploitation. The declines in populations of large marine species and in the health of marine ecosystems such as coral reefs are so significant that the baseline today is very different from that of over 500 years ago, or even 100 years ago. Furthermore, in some cases, recovery of marine species and ecosystems from damage and over-exploitation is much slower than previously believed, perhaps because populations have fallen below critical thresholds, or have shifted to stable but less desirable states.

Figure 2.1   Map of ocean currents in the Western Indian Ocean

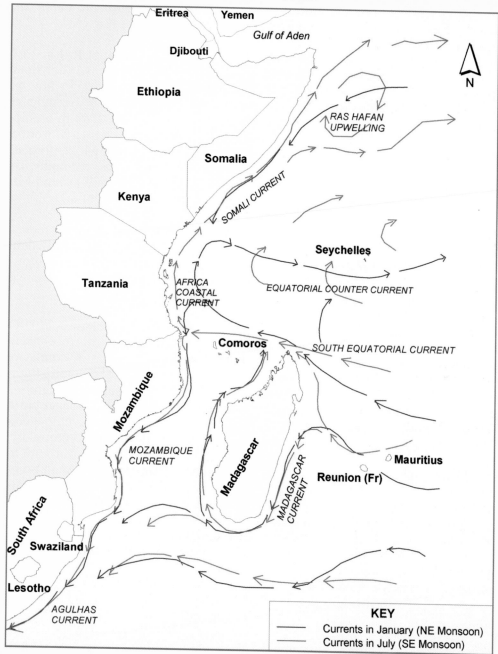

Tanzania's coastline lies at a key location in the West Indian Ocean. Ocean currents vary with the monsoons and provide an important physical link among all of the sites on the East African coast. The north-east monsoon (Kaskazi) predominates from November to March with gentle winds; the south-east monsoon blows from June to September with strong winds. The calmest periods are the inter-monsoons (March/April and October/November). The dominant current is the East African Coastal Current (EACC) which flows north along the Tanzanian coast. It flows fastest during the south-east monsoon meeting the East African coast at the latitude of Mtwara. During the north-east monsoon, the entire system shifts north and meets the mainland closer to the latitude of Mafia. The EACC affects primarily offshore waters but also causes down-welling resulting in a predominance of low nutrient, warm and clear water which encourages the extensive coral growth and benthic productivity associated with this coast.

URT can respond to this challenge by incorporating a system of MPAs and MMAs into the National Integrated Coastal Environment Management Strategy. Mainland Tanzania and Zanzibar have autonomous systems for addressing environmental issues including wildlife and fisheries. MPAs and other MMAs within the territorial seas are thus not a Union issue unless they are established in the wider EEZ.

Physical Characteristics

The ecological characteristics of an area depend on its physical characteristics, an understanding of which is vitally important when developing a system of MPAs and MMAs. Currents, which vary with the monsoons, are particularly important because they determine to a large extent how different sites are connected (Figure 2.1). Freshwater input from river outflow also contributes to linkages and connections and affects the distribution of species and habitats. In the URT, the impact of rivers such as the Rufiji, Pangani and Ruvuma is considerable. Peak outflow in April and May increases the amount of suspended sediments, and the sediment plumes from the Rufiji and Ruvuma River deltas stretch for many kilometers up the coastline. These are among the main reasons for reduced coral growth north of Mafia and south of Ras Matunda in Mtwara.

Key Ecosystems and Habitats

Coral Reefs. The coral reefs of URT cover an estimated 3 580 km², and are found along at least two thirds of the country's coastline. The areas of greatest concentration are Tanga, Pemba, Unguja, Mafia, the Songo Songo archipelago and Mtwara. Fringing and patch reefs predominate and are generally close to land because of the narrowness of the continental shelf.

Coral reefs prefer waters free from suspended sediments, excessive fresh water runoff, and pollutants, hence river mouths and estuaries tend to prevent their development. The turbid waters of the Rufiji River flow north, hence there is significantly less reef development along the northern mainland coast until the Tanga region, apart from fringing and patch reefs around the islands off Dar es Salaam. A complex string of patch and broken fringing reefs

stretches north from the northern part of Pangani district, to merge with the patch and fringing reef complex in southern Kenya.

South and east of the Rufiji Delta, where the continental shelf widens, the shallow waters of the Mafia and Songo Songo archipelagos support luxurious coral reefs. A fringing outer reef runs down the eastern side of both archipelagos to meet the mainland south of Kilwa Masoko, and from there it continues south to the Mozambique border, broken in places by deep water channels, river outlets and bays. The largest bays are around Mtwara and these support shallow patch reefs.

Unguja has a long fringing reef down the east coast and reefs fringe the small islands off the west coast. Reefs around Pemba are known to have been extensive and diverse, but are less well-studied than many other areas of URT.

Coral and reef fish diversities in URT are relatively high, but there has been little recent detailed taxonomic work. Some 140 species of corals were recorded in 1984. More recent coral diversity figures are available for individual sites such as Chumbe, Misali, Bawe, Mafia, Mnazi, and Songo Songo, but these need to be collated and analyzed to develop a general picture for the country. Of the reefs monitored by the Institute of Marine Science (IMS), those around Misali, Tutia and Mange off Mafia, and the Songo Songo Archipelago, are of high diversity. Chumbe is considered to have among the highest reef species diversity, but it is also one of the most intensively studied. Medium diversity is found on the reefs of Kunduchi, Stone Town, Menai Bay, Mnazi Bay, and Tanga region.

The current health of URT's reefs reflects a combination of factors that have had significant impacts on coral cover and species abundance and diversity over recent decades. The closeness of the reefs to land make them particularly prone to human impact, either from exploitation or indirect terrestrial influences such as pollution. Overall, reef health is probably quite good. The most degraded coral reefs appear to be those in shallow depths (less than 10 m), especially near urban centers such as Tanga, Dar es Salaam, and Mtwara. More pristine reefs are found in less accessible stretches of the coast and at greater depths; such as those around Kilwa, Mafia, and the Songo Songo archipelago.

Key factors determining reef health are destructive fishing methods and coral bleaching; both caused severe damage in the 1990s but many reefs are slowly recovering. The coral bleaching event of 1997/1998, triggered by El Nino, reduced average live hard coral from 52 percent to 26 percent. Corals on shallow reefs were most affected. The sites monitored by IMS showed high mortality (60-90 percent) on the outer reefs on the south-eastern side of Mafia (Tutia, Juani and Mange) and around Misali. Medium to high mortality occurred on the reefs around Mnazi Bay, Songo Songo, and Kunduchi (north of Dar es Salaam). The least affected reefs were those around Unguja with 10-25 percent mortality, perhaps due to the intrusion of cold water in mid-March. The impacts of bleaching were not uniform, but recovery everywhere has been very slow. However, the dead structure is still largely intact, and some level of recovery has been observed at all sites.

In some MPAs and MMAs, such as those in Muheza, Tanga and Pangani districts, much of the destructive fishing has been stopped, particularly dynamiting. Although it still tends to resurface periodically, as does illegal beach seining and other damaging methods. In other parts of the country, it is still a serious problem. A more localized problem, although having a major impact where it occurs, is the mining of live corals from reefs to make lime. This has been a particular issue in Mafia and Mtwara districts (both of which have been making considerable efforts to halt it) and in the Dar es Salaam area.

Mangroves. Eight species of mangrove are found in mainland Tanzania and ten occur in Zanzibar. Recent estimates indicate that the mainland mangroves cover about 108 000 ha, and those on Zanzibar cover about 18 000 ha (6 000 ha in Unguja and 12 000 ha in Pemba). On the mainland, in 1990, mangrove cover was estimated at 112 000 ha. Over the following decade, decreased coverage in some mainland areas was offset by increases elsewhere for a net loss of about 3 percent. Coverage increased slightly in Tanga, Muheza, Pangani, Bagamoyo, Dar es Salaam, Lindi and Mtwara districts, while decreases were noted in Rufiji, Kilwa, and Mkuranga districts. The small overall decline and the recovery noted in many areas is attributed to local initiatives fostering awareness and replanting, such as those in the Tanga region, and to the Mangrove Management

Project which protects and manages all mangroves as forest reserves. The latter may have caused a reduction in the amount of clearance for agriculture, salt pan construction, and coastal development.

Mangroves are found in all coastal districts, from Tanga to Mtwara, concentrated on gently sloping shores, river mouths, estuaries, creeks and bays. The largest continuous mangrove forests are in the districts of Tanga, Muheza, Rufiji, Kilwa, and Mtwara. The Rufiji Delta supports the largest mangrove forest (53 000 ha) in Eastern Africa. Other large mangrove stands occur at the estuaries of the major rivers such as Pangani, Wami, Ruvu, Matandu, Mbwemkuru and Ruvuma rivers; and well developed mangrove forests are found on Mafia Island. Much of the Pemba coastline is fringed with mangroves. On Unguja, the largest area is around Chwaka Bay.

Mangrove condition varies from locality to locality, and is primarily related to the extent to which the forests have been cut for domestic use (firewood, houses, fences, boats, fish traps and medicine) or commercial use (timber, fuel for lime production). There has been a severe deterioration of mangrove quality near urban centers such as Maruhubi in Zanzibar, Kunduchi, Mbweni and Mtoni in Dar es Salaam, and in forests around Tanga municipality. Less accessible areas in Rufiji district are in better condition. Mangroves on Pemba and Unguja are subject to intense cutting in several localities, particularly on Unguja.

Photo Peeva Eliste

Sea grass beds. Sea grasses are marine flowering plants that are adapted to live submerged in shallow waters and estuaries from the mid-tide mark to a depth of 20 m or more, where water quality allows sufficient sunlight to penetrate for photosynthesis. Twelve of the 50 species of sea grass that are found worldwide occur in URT. Usually several sea grass species occur together in mixed vegetation that forms extensive meadows; these stands may be very dynamic, their position being determined by the frequency of exposure, and sediment grain size and movement.

The area covered by sea grass beds and species densities in URT is unknown. Sea grass beds are widely distributed in inter-tidal and sub-tidal mud and sand flats and sand bars, in coastal lagoons, in sandy areas around the bases of shallow, patch and fringing reefs, and in mangrove creeks exposed to low tide. They are found in abundance in sheltered areas of the coast in Tanga, the tidal zones fronting the deltas of Ruvu, Wami and Rufiji rivers and around Kilwa. They also occur in Pemba, Unguja and Mafia islands.

Sea grass beds can be damaged by natural and human activities that include illegal fishing methods (beach seining and shallow water trawling), regular anchoring of fishing and tourist boats, excessive sedimentation which increases turbidity and reduces light penetration, shoreline dynamics, and predation by sea urchins and dugongs. The extent to which these threats pose a problem in URT requires study.

Other Habitats. Descriptions of homogenous and very distinct habitats such as coral reefs, mangroves, and sea grass beds tend to give the impression that the coastal and marine environment can be easily categorized into particular types of habitat. In fact, much of it is a mosaic of small areas dominated by many different community types. Cliffs, rocky shores, islands, beaches, estuaries, tidal flats, and offshore habitats are all important to the overall ecological functioning of the coastal environment, but they are often difficult to quantify or map.

Key Species

Dugong. The dugong is one of the most endangered species on the African continent and is almost extinct in URT. It is in Appendix 1 of CITES and is on the IUCN Red List as Vulnerable. Information on its distribution and abundance in URT is scarce and is mainly in the form of anecdotal reports and incidental sightings. Records since 2000 suggest that 8-10 dugongs are killed annually for their meat and oil, but accidental entanglement and drowning in gillnets occurs often. Other threats include degradation of sea grass beds, its main food supply.

Dugongs were reported to be relatively abundant and widely distributed prior to the mid-1970s, with incidental gillnet capture of 3-5 animals per day. Now they are very rare, with only 32 sightings in the whole country between January 2000 and May 2003. The first nation-wide assessment (in 2003) together with on-going research on Mafia and the capture of an individual in a fishing net in January 2004 indicates the existence of a small and threatened population in the Mafia-Rufiji-Kilwa area. Between Jaja in Rufiji and Somanga in Kilwa, this is probably the largest remaining concentration in the country. Other relatively recent sightings occurred near Moa in Muheza district, and in the northern part of Pemba.

In the Rufiji–Kilwa area dugong move close to the shore during the cooler months of May-August (south-east monsoon) when sea temperatures are low. They return to deeper waters during the warmer months of November-February (north-east monsoon).

Some Less Charismatic Coastal Habitats in Mainland Tanzania and Zanzibar.

Cliffs and Rocky Shores. *Much of the coastline is formed of low (4 m high) limestone coral cliffs. Some of these areas also include coralline islets, which are fossilized coral reefs. The cliffs and islets were formed when reefs were built during the Pleistocene era – 130 000 years ago – and subsequently exposed by a drop in sea level. Fossilized coral reefs extend up to one km inland in some places.*

Islands. *URT has numerous small islands dotted along the coast, particularly where the continental shelf widens. Most of these islands are uninhabited although they may be used frequently by fishermen for camping; in populated areas they are increasingly being used for recreation and tourism. Many (particularly those off Pemba and Unguja) have remnants of natural coastal forest with endemic species (e.g., duikers, coconut crabs). The most remote is Latham Island (<3 ha in area), a weathered fossil coral island.*

Beaches. *Sandy beaches are a predominant feature of the coast of URT. Much of the mainland coast and the eastern shore of Unguja is lined with beaches. Sandy beaches tend to be very dynamic ecosystems and in many parts of the country they change markedly with the season or through natural longer-term processes of accretion and erosion. These processes can be greatly accentuated by human activities such as sand mining and coastal construction and engineering activities.*

Estuaries. *Rivers influence the coast and marine environment by discharging water, sediments, nutrients and pollutants, and creating productive brackish water environments in estuaries. They also contribute to the maintenance of deltas, tidal flats and shorelines, and to the nourishment of mangroves and sea grass beds. The peak outflow from the rivers corresponds to the coastal rainfall pattern and occurs between March and May. Most estuaries have brackish water swamps or mudflats, and are often lined with mangrove trees/forests. Estuaries and shallow bays are of critical importance as nursery and spawning areas for many commercial fish species; for example, the importance of the Bagamoyo area on the mainland, and Chwaka Bay on Unguja, is illustrated by the fact that most of the catches in these areas comprise immature fish. River mouths and estuaries are also key habitats for prawns, and the surrounding areas are key prawn fishing grounds.*

Tidal Flats. *Much of the shore is dominated by mud and saline flats which are important feeding areas for birds. While these saline habitats have few large organisms, they often harbor abundant invertebrate life, particularly if they are regularly inundated.*

Offshore Habitats. *There is very little information for most of the 200 000 km^2 EEZ. Some surveys of benthic habitats have been carried out, and a recent multi-national bathymetric survey, led by South African scientists, has found that deep water canyons (typical habitat of the coelacanth) fringe much of the continental shelf of mainland Tanzania, particularly in the south. The offshore waters are generally less productive than, for example, those in Western Africa, largely due to the lack of upwellings. Productivity varies seasonally as it is dependent on phytoplankton which flourish when waters are warm; this in turn influences the distribution of large pelagic fish (such as tuna, king fish and marlin) and results in the seasonality of fisheries for these species. But the relationships between fish stocks, temperature and phytoplankton in URT has yet to be studied; such research requires relatively sophisticated technology including satellite information.*

Birds in Tanzania.

Important Bird Areas (IBAs), *designated by Birdlife International through a widely accepted scientific process, provide an indication of priority bird conservation areas. 10 IBAs have been designated along the coast:*

Tanga North (IBA 35) – *Kibo salt pans, south-west of Moa village; surveyed only once but showed important populations of greater sandplovers and curlew sandpipers.*

Tanga South (IBA 36) – *south of Mtangata Bay; salt pans, beach and mangroves important for greater sandplovers and crab plovers.*

Dar es Salaam (IBA 21) – *inter-tidal mud flat (up to 25 km² in area), with salt pans, mangroves, river inlets and small islets; tidal range of up to 4 m; important for crab plovers, roseate terns, Saunders terns and numerous migrants in the northern winter.*

Rufiji Delta (IBA 32) – *recognized locally and internationally as an important wintering ground for migrant birds and likely to be important for numerous wetland and water birds, but poorly known.*

Mafia Island (IBA 12) – *provides staging ground for various palearctic migrant species; Mafia MP in particular provides feeding grounds for a variety of wading birds; is also a nesting area for open-billed storks and fish eagles.*

Mnazi Bay (IBA 28) – *important area for migratory birds with salt pans and mangroves on small islands that provide major wader roosts.*

Zanzibar South Coast (IBA 44) – *important roseate tern colony on small islet off Chumbe Island; crab plovers and terek sandpipers and other waders in Kiwani and Kombeni Bays.*

Zanzibar East Coast (IBA 45) – *Chwaka Bay is a key area for crab plovers and greater sand plovers; up to 15 percent of the world population of Saunders tern may winter here.*

Pemba (IBA 76) – *mainly important for endemic terrestrial species but large number of dimorphic egrets and crab plovers observed and the mangroves may provide important bird roost and feeding grounds.*

Latham Island (IBA 27) – *critical importance for its masked booby colony, and also an important breeding site for sooty terns, brown noddies, swift terns, and black-naped terns; considered the most important seabird island off the coast of East Africa.*

Other Marine Mammals. There is little information on other marine mammals in URT. Eight species of dolphin have been recorded and are often caught accidentally in tuna/billfish/marlin nets, particularly off Nungwi (Unguja). The most common species are the Indo-Pacific bottlenose dolphin, the Indo-Pacific humpback dolphin, and the spinner dolphin. Menai Bay has a significant population of 150 resident bottlenose and 75 humpback dolphins. Humpback and other whale species pass through Tanzanian waters on migration and may calve in Mnazi Bay.

Birds. A wide variety of coastal birds and seabirds are found in URT, particularly in mangrove forests, inter-tidal flats, and on rocky cliffs. Open water areas such as the Zanzibar and Mafia channels and the Indian Ocean itself provide rich feeding grounds for true seabirds such as terns, gannets, brown noddies and boobies. Waders and shorebirds visit URT in large numbers each year between August and May to feed, particularly on inter-tidal flats at low tides.

Marine Turtles. All five species of sea turtles found in the WIO occur in URT waters: the green turtle and the hawksbill turtle are the most common; the olive ridley, loggerhead and leatherback turtles are also occasionally seen. They are threatened by habitat destruction, over harvesting for meat and eggs, incidental capture in gillnets, and disturbance of nesting beaches because of construction.

Other Marine Species. There is very little information available on fish and invertebrates. The most comprehensive survey of reef fish was for Mafia where almost 400 species were recorded. Chumbe and other well-managed sites in the region had larger fish and higher diversity fish populations than fished reefs such as those off Dar and in Tanga. Rare and threatened fish species need to be considered in the development of an MPA network. These include the coelacanth which was recently discovered in URT when a specimen was caught by a fisherman in the Kilwa area. Seahorses are a group that is an indicator of the health of sea grass beds; many species are under threat globally. Seahorses are known to occur in Mafia, Songo Songo and Mnazi Bay. They warrant further attention. Sharks are poorly known but are also thought to be declining in URT. MPAs and MMAs may be important tools for conserving remaining stocks. Similarly, recent attention has been drawn to the global decline in fish spawning aggregation sites, and the role that MPAs can play in protecting these. Certain species congregate in large aggregations to spawn, often around a topographic feature such as a reef outcrop or headland that provides a refuge from currents. No published information is available on such sites for URT, but anecdotal evidence suggests that Songo Songo and Mafia may be important areas.

Equally little is known about the status and distribution of invertebrates. The threatened coconut crab is an indicator of relatively undisturbed areas, and occurs on Misali and Chumbe and probably other small islands. Sea cucumbers have drastically declined throughout the inshore waters of URT, and MPAs may be their last refugia. Many of the commercial species of mollusks are over-exploited, both for food and their shells.

Current and Proposed MPAs

Table 1.2 provides a summary of all marine management areas in the URT.

Mainland Tanzania. Legislation for mainland Tanzania allows for the gazetting of three types of MPA: Marine Parks, Marine Reserves, and National Parks containing marine habitat. The Marine Parks and Reserves Act of 1994 allows for the designation of Marine Parks and Marine Reserves which are managed by the Marine Parks and Reserves Unit.

Marine Parks (MPs): relatively large multiple-use zoned MPAs, of which two have been gazetted: Mafia Island MP (Mafia district) and Mnazi Bay-Ruvuma Estuary MP (Mtwara district).

Marine Reserves (MRs): smaller areas in which extraction of any marine resource is prohibited. Several MRs were gazetted in the 1970s, some of which have now been incorporated into other management arrangements. There are now two MR areas: Maziwe Island MR (Pangani district) and the Dar es Salaam MR System which comprises 4 separately designated MRs (Bongoyo, Fungu Yasini, Mgudya and Pangavini) managed as a single system. Discussions are underway about designating all small islands as Reserves; this is general policy at present as far as the terrestrial part of an island is concerned, but further discussions will be held before legislation is introduced, and before consideration is given to including marine waters.

The Wildlife Conservation Act of 1974 allows for the designation of National Parks (which prohibit exploitation) and Game Reserves. These are managed by the Tanzania National Parks Authority (TANAPA). The proposed Saadani National Park (straddling Bagamoyo and Pangani districts) is currently a Game Reserve, and when re-gazetted

Photo: Dean Housden

will include a marine extension which makes it the first National Park to include marine habitat. The implementation arrangements for marine areas within National Parks have yet to be determined.

Zanzibar. In Zanzibar, the overall mandate for protected areas lies with the Ministry of Agriculture, Natural Resources, Environment and Co-operatives (MANREC). Two main approaches to protected area management have evolved: co-management arrangements between local communities and the government (Misali Island, Menai Bay and Kiwengwa); and agreements with tourism companies that manage lodges within the MPAs (Chumbe Island and Mnemba Island). Three pieces of legislation provide for protected area establishment.

The Environmental Management for Sustainable Development Act (Environment Act) of 1996 addresses protected areas in general and defines categories: Controlled Areas (subsequently referred to as Conservation Areas), Reserves, Parks, and Sanctuaries. Under this Act, the following falls under the mandate of the Department of Commercial Crops, Fruits and Forestry (DCCFF):

Jozani National Park (established in 2004).

Ngezi Forest Nature Reserve will include beach and mangrove habitat (proposed).

The Forest Resources Management Act of 1996 provides for the gazetting of Forest Reserves:

Jozani Forest Reserve (Unguja) was gazetted in 1996 and the area now includes inter-tidal habitat after being regazetted as a National Park.

Ngezi Forest Reserve (Pemba) includes mangrove forest and beach (but no sub-tidal habitat), gazetted in 1959 but with no real protection until the 1990s.

All mangroves are gazetted as forest reserves.

The Fisheries Act of 1988 allows for the establishment of MPAs. The following have been gazetted and are under the mandate of the Department of Fisheries and Marine Products:

Chumbe Island was gazetted as a no-take Sanctuary in 1994. The forest is protected as a "closed forest." Management is delegated to a private company – Chumbe Island Coral Park Limited (CHICOP) – which has developed the tourism lodge on the island under two separate agreements with the government, one for the marine sanctuary (1994-2004) and a second for the forest (1994-2027).

Kiwengwa Controlled Area (Unguja) was established in 2000 but was never managed. It was previously an important turtle nesting area.

Mnemba Island Marine Conservation Area (MIMCA) was initially protected in 1992, extending 200 m offshore around Mnemba Island as a no-take area. Formal gazetting in 2002 extended the area to include the whole reef. This no-take area is co-managed with Conservation Corporation Africa, which runs the tourism lodge on Mnemba Island. MIMCA has recently expanded to cover much of the eastern coast of Unguja including the Kiwengwa Controlled Area and Chwaka Bay.

Menai Bay Conservation Area was gazetted in 1997. Regulated fishing is allowed. It is managed with support from WWF and in collaboration with the local villages.

Misali Island Marine Conservation Area is a no-take zone gazetted in 1998. The forest is protected under the Forest Resources Management Act, and is managed jointly by the Misali Island Conservation Association (MICA) and the DCCFF.

Turtles in Tanzania.

All species of sea turtles are listed on Appendix 1 of CITES; the green turtle, olive ridley and loggerhead are categorized by IUCN as Endangered; the leatherback and hawksbill are classified as Critically Endangered. In 1988 there was a nesting population of about 300 green turtles. There are thought to be only about 50 hawksbill nests annually (20 used to nest on the main rookery, Maziwe, before it became a sandbank and regularly submerged on high tides). The olive ridley is a rare visitor nesting in small numbers.

Current and Proposed Marine and Coastal Management Areas

Mangrove Forest Reserves and collaborative mangrove management areas. On the mainland, all mangroves are gazetted as Forest Reserves under the forestry legislation; the amended Act (2002) provides for their joint management by local communities and the Mangrove Management Unit of the Forest and Beekeeping Division of MNRT. The Reserves are zoned according to the uses allowed, and those designated as "core zones" might technically qualify as protected areas. In other zones, controlled harvesting of poles (selective cutting) is permitted where mangroves are ecologically stable and have sufficient regeneration potential. A collaborative mangrove management plan has been prepared under the Tanga Programme for mangroves in Pangani district, but has yet to be implemented. For administrative and planning purposes, mangroves have been divided into ten blocks grouped into three units. The northern unit includes the blocks of Tanga, Muheza, Pangani and Bagamoyo districts. The central unit includes Dar es Salaam, Mkuranga, Mafia and Rufiji districts while the southern unit includes Kilwa, Lindi and Mtwara districts.

Collaborative fisheries management areas. Six such areas have been established in the three northern districts (Tanga, Muheza, Pangani) through the Tanga Coastal Zone Conservation and Development Program (TCZCDP), and are implemented jointly by local villages and the districts. The boundaries of these areas are determined by ascertaining the use of the area by a group of villages; they are therefore based on resource use rather than biodiversity characteristics or administrative arrangements (two of the areas cross district boundaries). Selected reefs within the six fisheries management areas have been closed by the villages to fishing (one of these areas is Maziwe Island MR). The institutional and legal framework for the management areas is still being finalized, but the plans for each area are approved at the national level by the Fisheries Department and legal backing is provided by village and district bylaws.

National Integrated Coastal Management Initiatives

The National Integrated Coastal Environment Management Strategy (NICEMS) currently provides a structure that supports the concept of establishing an ecological system of management areas. This strategy addresses mainland Tanzania; Zanzibar is also considering an Integrated Coastal Management (ICM) approach to coastal resource management. NICEMS contains a number of sub-strategies that are of relevance to the development of marine areas:

Support for environmental planning and integrated management of coastal resources. This is to be achieved through the establishment of district ICM action plans, for which guidelines have been prepared. The plans may cover the full district and offshore waters to the seaward edge of the territorial waters, but could also be for smaller areas within the district such as a village or a bay. On the mainland, pilots are being developed at Pangani, Bagamoyo, Kinondoni, Mkuranga, and Rufiji. The Pangani ICM is linked with the two collaborative fishery management areas in this district under the TCZCDP. The Kinondoni Integrated Coastal Area Management Program (KICAMP) was set up in 2000 to develop a local ICM strategy, and includes part of the Dar es Salaam MR system. On Zanzibar, the Environment Act allows for national ICM planning and village level ICM plans, coordinated by the Department of Environment. There is one demonstration site at the Chwaka Bay-Paje area where a Coastal Resource Management Committee has been established as an activity related to the development of the new National Park.

Biodiversity conservation. This proposes that integrated conservation should be undertaken using the Marine Parks and Marine Reserves Act, the Mangrove Management Program, parks and reserves as defined under the Wildlife Act, and wetlands and fragile lands as defined under the Land Act. The Town and Country Planning Ordinance Cap 378 also identifies sensitive ecosystems for conservation including beaches, mangroves, coral reefs, estuaries, deltas, and coastal mudflats. The district ICM Action Plans and Special Area Management Plans (SAMPs) identify locally important critical coastal areas and areas of high biodiversity, and specify actions that provide for their conservation, restoration and sustainable use by coastal residents.

Targeted planning for high value and high vulnerability systems. This proposes an integrated planning and management mechanism for coastal areas of high economic value or with substantial environmental vulnerability. The approach is based on the concept of SAMPs, applied to one or more districts, or simply an area within a district. These areas are developed as a partnership arrangement between central and local governments, with local stakeholder input.

Integrated planning is also important in the context of potential tourism, hydrocarbon, mining, and mariculture development within national and local plans and strategies:

🦆 The URT Tourism Master Plan (2003) for the mainland classifies much of the coast within tourism zones. Coastal tourism is being prioritized because the northern wildlife areas – Serengeti and Kilimanjaro – are becoming over-crowded and there is now increased interest in diversification and spreading the benefits. Whereas in 1988 there were no hotels on the east coast of Unguja, by 2000 there were some 22. Implementation of the tourism plans for both the mainland and Zanzibar will need to take into account the distribution

Photo Indu Hewawasam

and status of sandy beaches, and of coral reefs in particular, both of which are key resources for tourists. The Tourism Master Plan for the mainland emphasizes the role that MPAs might play in the successful expansion of the tourism industry.

🦆 Oil is actively being explored on Nunyi (south of Mafia), in the Rufiji Delta, and south of Kilwa. The Songo Songo gas pipeline designed to carry gas directly to Dar es Salaam has now been completed; a long-term environmental monitoring program has been initiated with plans for associated conservation activities. Gas is also to be piped from Mnazi Bay – within the Marine Park – to Mtwara. The Marine Park is working closely with the companies involved to identify how operations can be carried out without harm to the area, and to develop ways by which the Park itself might benefit from this operation.

🦆 Areas of the coast given over to mariculture and salt production provide important sources of revenue for many coastal villages. Seaweed farming is carried out in numerous sites, predominantly on the east coast of Unguja, in the three northern districts of the Tanga region, around Mafia, and in the Kilwa/Songo-Songo area. If managed carefully, seaweed mariculture

Much of the theoretical basis for "how much should be protected" is based on current understanding of the role of no-take or exclusion areas in maintaining biodiversity and fishery biomass. Recent scientific studies suggest that networks of fully protected (no-extraction) MPAs should cover 20 percent or more of all biogeographic regions and habitats; benefits from such MPAs may be maximized when 20-50 percent of habitat is protected.

areas could be linked within a network of other management areas, as is being done with the collaborative fishery management areas in Muheza, Tanga and Pangani districts. The small-scale salt works along the coast rely on solar evaporation and involve small numbers of people and very little equipment. If managed appropriately, these areas could provide both long-term employment for local communities and suitable bird habitat; they host some 300 000 migrant coastal waders, and form a vital component of the habitat preferred by migrants for feeding and safe roosting at high tide.

Goals of a System

The previous sections show that while some managed areas are in place, not all ecosystems and species of interest are managed sustainably. If URT is to move beyond the current situation, a clearer system is required that reflects the following ecosystem goals in network and system design:

Representativeness. To ensure that all types of biodiversity (both species and habitats) receive protection.

Comprehensiveness and Adequacy. To recognize the full range of species and ecosystems to be included, and to ensure that the individual components are of sufficient size and appropriate spatial distribution to promote the ecological viability and integrity of populations and species.

Connectivity. To ensure linkages between individual components.

Resilience. To ensure that the network can survive natural catastrophes and major impacts, by replicating sites that have particularly vulnerable species and ecosystems (e.g., coral reefs).

Representativeness

This means ensuring that the selected areas reflect the biodiversity of the whole area. A representative network needs to include: all ecosystem/habitat types, including those that are rare or particularly vulnerable; all species and characteristic species communities; critical habitat for threatened, restricted range or endemic species; and areas important for vulnerable life stages, such as spawning aggregations, breeding sites and migration routes. For example, current MPA coverage in Eastern Africa, including URT, is not representative; there is a clear bias towards protection of coral reefs, compared with mangroves and coastal wetlands.

Comprehensiveness and Adequacy

Comprehensiveness means recognizing all types of ecosystems in a given area, and adequacy means ensuring that ecosystems are of sufficient size and appropriate spatial distribution to ensure the ecological viability and integrity of populations and species. Deciding how many MPAs are required and how large these should be is a major challenge in designing a network. The basic principle should be that the network is large enough to cover the full range of ecosystems or habitats in the area, preferably with multiple samples of each. Meeting this goal implies that the total amount of ocean gazetted as MPAs is less important than whether appropriate amounts of each habitat type are included.

The disadvantages of small sites are that they may only function if essential linkages to other habitats are maintained; they are more vulnerable to disturbances such as low tides or algal blooms; and populations of some species need a large area to be sustainable. The size of an MPA also influences management effectiveness. Small areas are often easier to set up, enforce, and monitor, and good relationships with stakeholders are easier to develop. Larger areas take much longer to set up, will be more costly, and will require much greater investment in developing relationships with the inevitably larger number of stakeholders.

Connectivity

An MPA network could be designed to encompass full representation of all marine biodiversity but it would not necessarily recognize connectivity between coastal and marine ecosystems, and thus might not conserve ecological functioning and system productivity. Connectivity among MPAs, and between MPAs and other areas, is very important given the characteristics of marine organisms (larval dispersal, reproduction through spawning, pelagic juveniles and adults) and of the marine environment (mixing of waters through wind, currents, tides, and upwellings). Sediments, nutrients, plankton, animals, and pollution are re-distributed from their original sources up and down coastlines and across oceans, and different habitats are closely connected by the species that move between them. A network must therefore take into account:

- Exchange of offspring between populations through larval dispersal.

- Movement of juveniles and adults between the MPAs and other sites.

- Ecosystem linkages through transfer of materials such as organic carbon.

Information relating to these factors is extremely limited or even absent in URT but it is useful to look at each factor to see what might be involved as the network evolves.

Larval dispersal. The extent to which larvae are exchanged between MPAs, or dispersed out of or into MPAs, will depend on their dispersal distances, local oceanography (especially currents), and the distances between an MPA and other MPAs or sites relevant to the species life history. For most species, there is no information on how fast or how far their larvae travel, and for those for which there are data, there is great variation in dispersal characteristics. An MPA network that might suit the dispersal of one species is unlikely

to be suitable for all others. If larvae survive for a long time, this does not necessarily mean that they travel long distances. However, those that do travel far may play key roles in maintaining gene flow with populations at the extreme end of the species range. Isolated MPAs will benefit from larvae with short dispersal ranges as they will be retained within the area. Ideally, information on larval dispersal distance is needed as it will help to dictate the size of individual units within a network, as well as how far apart they should be spaced. This information is lacking for all groups of species in URT at present, but information on currents suggests that both Mnazi Bay and the Mafia/Songo Songo area may be important source areas, as these are the points where, depending on the monsoon, the EACC divides, and flows north along the rest of the URT coastline.

Movement of adults and juveniles. The URT provides breeding and feeding areas for a range of migratory species including marine mammals, birds, turtles, and fish. Turtles are known to migrate large distances; tags have been recovered from turtles found in Mafia and Zanzibar, that were tagged when nesting in Seychelles, Comoros, and South Africa. A tagged turtle from Mida Creek in Kenya was recently found in Mnazi Bay. Tagged sharks have also been found to travel long distances in the Western Indian Ocean, and billfish and large schools of tuna migrate each year. This illustrates that national or even regional level MPA networks may not be able to

protect all the key sites for particular species, and it emphasizes the need for ensuring that appropriate transboundary linkages are made.

Linkages between different ecosystems. It is known that turtles and some reef fish, snappers for example, require both sea grasses and reef habitats at different life stages. Transfer of nutrients between certain ecosystems is also important. Nutrients from the Ruvuma River estuary have been shown to be responsible for sustaining the Mozambique prawn fishery to the south. Small MPAs may therefore only be sustainable if interdependent patches of habitat occur nearby, with the same level of protection. In the URT, the larger MPAs include several linked habitats, and all the MPAs include land as well as a range of sub-tidal habitat.

Resilience

Habitats that are especially vulnerable to disturbance need special attention. These often depend on biological or living structures – such as coral reefs and mangroves – and disturbance of the structure risks destroying entire ecological communities. Coral reefs have been most studied in the context of resilience because the extent to which they are affected by high sea surface temperatures is variable. The intensity of bleaching, the species affected, the depth, and the extent of mortality all vary according to where a reef is located, and the local conditions affecting it.

Resilience is addressed when developing MPA networks by spreading the risk of damage or extinction. In practical terms, this means that habitat types are replicated in the network so that if one MPA is eliminated, others stay intact. This redundancy is reinforced through good connectivity; sites that survive a particular impact can provide a source of replenishment for those that have been damaged.

URT has many reefs highly susceptible to bleaching as demonstrated during the 1997/98 El Nino. Data from monitoring after the event might help to guide establishment of new MPAs or management of existing ones. For example, reefs off Stone Town in Zanzibar and in Chole Bay in Mafia Marine Park largely escaped bleaching. In the case of Chole Bay, it is believed that this is because the extensive shallow

inter-tidal areas in the bay cool down at night and thus lower overall temperatures. Locations such as Misali and Tutia reef which experienced extensive bleaching have no such areas.

Future bleaching events should be carefully documented so that data on resilient and resistant reefs are made available and can be incorporated into MPA network design. The network should also allow not only for protection of resilient reefs, but also for recovery of those that have been damaged by bleaching. Recovery could involve active restoration by, for example, the transplantation of corals. An equally important but longer term approach is the promotion of natural recovery by reducing or eliminating other reef threats, such as destructive fishing practices.

Scale, Precaution and Adaptiveness

From an ecological perspective, the factors and conditions described above can be translated into some operational principles. In general, we again stress that the term system "design" can be somewhat of a misnomer in that it implies that we can carefully plan and select all attributes. The previous discussions illustrated that, in the first place, we do not have a comprehensive information base on which to make such decisions and, even if we did, the conditions themselves change in response to external factors over which we have little control.

System design thus boils down to an attempt to reflect, at all stages of evolution, the following principles:

- Sufficient Scale. This comes from the ideas of connectivity, comprehensiveness and adequacy. In selecting priority networks, and an over-arching system for these networks, we will choose to err on the side of too large a scale. Over a fifty-year time horizon, as more information becomes available, networks and other sub-systems can thus be prioritized. As with sustainable development, the idea is to maintain options for future generations; this means not foreclosing on potential opportunities.

- Precautionary Measures. The precautionary principle applies well to systems that need to be resilient and representative. Redundancy is an important concept within a precautionary approach, as is diversity. Redundancy does not necessarily mean idleness; it can be reflected through the duplication of processes, the use of back-up systems, or application of repetitive parallel procedures that seek to achieve the same (or a comparable) goal. While traditional ideas may have shunned duplication, decisions taken under uncertainty can and should accommodate back-up plans and safety nets.

- Adaptive Mechanisms. A persistent theme in describing ecosystem behavior is that such systems adapt. Any system that attempts to manage ecosystems must therefore itself also be flexible and able to adapt to changing circumstances. Much of the adaptability comes more from the management mechanisms rather than from any inherent aspect of system design. Multi-stakeholder systems that share responsibilities, through adaptive co-management, are an example of such adaptive mechanisms.

Some Alternatives

In arriving at the Blueprint 2050 Vision, a number of alternatives were considered in developing a system of marine protection. Because Blueprint 2050 captures some aspects of all of these alternatives, we here review them in some greater detail. They include systems that focus on: (i) species protection; (ii) habitat protection; and, (iii) fisheries management areas.

Species-Based Protection

Species are one logical starting point for a network because they are most easily understood. Many of the existing MPAs were established to protect threatened or other key species, largely a result of early analyses of the distribution of marine biodiversity. Turtles and dugong are good examples. Marine turtle nesting beaches are among the reasons for the establishment of the MPAs of Maziwe, Mafia, the proposed Saadani National Park, Kiwengwa, Misali, and Mnemba. Remnant dugong populations also figured in the establishment of the Mafia Island, and the Mnazi Bay-Ruvuma Estuary Marine Parks.

The establishment of dugong sanctuaries in key sites of the Muheza district is currently recommended.

A system targeting endangered, threatened, or ecologically important species can have the conservation of biological diversity at its core, albeit at a more restricted level than a fully representative system. Such a system could be part of a management strategy for protecting threatened species; or could be developed as a proxy or surrogate for more comprehensive protection of marine biodiversity. In the latter case, the species chosen to form the basis of the system would have to be an umbrella species; i.e., species with relatively broad ecological requirements whose conservation usually requires protection of habitats on which many other species depend. For example, the survival of the hawksbill turtle depends on coral reefs on which it feeds and sandy beaches on which it nests, and its successful protection potentially leads to protection of many other species.

A network aimed at threatened marine species would comprise MPAs covering the critical habitats of the key selected species, the transboundary connections that are needed to support them, and would be designed to address the specific threats affecting the species at each site. Critical habitats such as upwelling areas and other feeding zones, shallow water banks, and key migration points would need to be included. Since the species would move between the different sites in the network, these linking "corridors" would also need some form of protection, although perhaps not in a geographical sense; for example, prohibiting exploitation would help to ensure that the species could still move between the different parts of the network.

URT could adopt the species approach more comprehensively by targeting a suite of marine and coastal species including marine turtles, humpback whales, dugong, selected species within coral reef, sea grass, and mangrove habitats, and possibly offshore pelagic species like yellowfin tuna. The disadvantage of this approach is that potentially it would miss important biodiversity sites; for example, if the hawksbill turtle were selected, its population and range within URT is so small that very few sites would be included; if the green turtle were selected, key habitats, such as coral reefs, would be excluded.

The East African Marine Ecoregion (EAME) programme is a WWF led initiative to develop a long-term "50 year conservation vision" and strategic plan for the sustainable management of this region's marine resources. As part of its work, key sites for biodiversity conservation have already been identified. The identification process used four key habitats/community groups to assess the relative importance of different areas:

- *Coral communities and associated fauna.*

- *Mangrove communities.*

- *Sea grass, algae and sponge communities.*

- *Wetlands, coastal lakes, inland pools, sandy shores and dunes.*

Examining these groups, EAME reconnaissance identified seven priority seascapes in the URT. Four are on the mainland: Msambweni-Tanga; Bagamoyo; Rufiji-Mafia Complex; and, Mtwara-Quirimbas. The other three comprise Unguja, Pemba, and Latham islands. The Rufiji and Mtwara areas are considered globally important, while the remainder are ecoregionally or sub-regionally important.

All of these areas, except Latham Island, have some modest protection:

- *Both globally important areas have MPAs, covering 7 percent of the seascape in the case of Mafia and 2 percent in the case of Mnazi Bay (in the Mtwara complex). The latter is a transboundary seascape.*

- *Of the three ecoregionally important areas with MPAs, Misali protects 0.5 percent of the Pemba priority seascape; MPAs on Unguja cover about 8.7 percent; and the closed areas within the collaborative fishery management areas contribute about 1 percent to protection of the Tanga seascape.*

- *Bagamoyo is a subregionally important priority area, and will receive about 8 percent protection when the Saadani National Park marine portion is established.*

Habitat-Based Protection

A system of MPAs based on areas of representative habitat ensures that higher level biological diversity is conserved, and prevents the common pitfall of protecting only one component of biodiversity. When there is more than one MPA containing each habitat type, the precautionary principle is employed effectively, and resilience is addressed. Multiple examples of a habitat increase the chances that at least one will be protected if poor management or natural catastrophe ruins one or more of the others.

A fully representative network requires that one or more MPAs is established for each habitat type and species group. For this to happen, a biogeographic classification of the coastal and marine environment is needed so that the location of all habitat types is known. These include coral reefs, small islands, mangroves, estuaries, deltas, beaches, sea grass beds, rock reefs, sea mounts, and offshore pelagic zones. As in many countries, URT does not yet have complete information on all marine biodiversity within its coastal zone and EEZ; considerable effort would be required to compile this because there has been no national marine biodiversity survey or mapping.

Consequently, little can be said about the extent to which the existing network of MPAs is representative. Reefs occur in all MPAs but the total amount protected is not known. However, most of the current no-take areas, totaling some 66 km², are predominantly coral reef. Based on this figure, about 2 percent of URT's coral reefs are totally protected, with a larger proportion subject to other management measures. Mangroves are all included in Forest Reserves but are less well represented in formal protected areas; for example, none of the Rufiji Delta is formally protected. For other habitats, data are not available to make an assessment of representativeness.

While some have asserted that protected areas have been created in the past on an ad hoc basis, there is a good correspondence between existing MPAs and MMAs, and the priority areas identified for biodiversity conservation by a reconnaissance under the EAME programme. Only one MPA – Dar es Salaam MR System – does not fall in an EAME seascape, but this was established largely for tourism and recreation, rather than biodiversity protection. This does not mean, however, that there are enough, or that they are large enough to ensure adequate representation, but it does indicate that existing MPAs form a sound baseline for the development of a representative system.

Fisheries Management Areas

Marine management areas of various types have traditionally been used in many countries to maintain fish stocks and their associated habitats. In Australia, for example, Fish Habitat Reserves are established under the fisheries legislation to protect key fishery habitats, such as estuaries and sea grass beds. Fishing is allowed in such areas but activities that will damage the habitat are prohibited. Other types of fishery management areas include those closed to specific gear types or to the take of certain species, either on a permanent, temporary or seasonal basis. In URT, at one level the whole coast could be considered a fisheries management area because it is covered by national legislation (enforced to a greater or lesser extent) that prohibits the use of certain gears and imposes a range of regulations. But the real level of protection and management is much less than this might suggest.

No-take Areas. The biggest issue surrounding the establishment of any fishery management area is the extent to which part of it should be closed to fishing. Scientific studies show that in many places species diversity, biomass, size of individuals, and abundance are higher inside no-take zones than outside, or higher after the area was designated as a no-take zone than before. Such studies also show that increases can occur within as short a time as three years. Biomass can in fact be double that found outside the boundaries. No-take areas are therefore being promoted in many countries. The most effective no-take areas are those that accommodate not only the movements of target fish, but are also developed with fishing communities to meet their needs.

In URT, there are several no-take areas covering some 66 km² and designated in different ways:

- Marine Reserves on the mainland (Dar es Salaam MR System, Maziwe MR).

- Core zones in Marine Parks (Mafia Island Marine Park where 1.8 percent of the total marine area is no-take).

- Closed reefs in the six collaborative Tanga fishery management areas cover 1.7 percent of the total managed area.

- Conservation Areas on Zanzibar (Chumbe, Mnemba, Misali).

Theory suggests that many such small no-take areas should be better for the export of larvae and adults to fishing grounds because of the large edge-to-area ratio. However, studies have shown that benefits are independent of size, and that the size effect probably depends on whether the species concerned are sedentary or mobile and, if mobile, how much they move. On the Great Barrier Reef, the minimum size calculated as being necessary for effective no-take areas is 20 km along the smallest linear axis. Elsewhere, a minimum of about 32 km has been suggested, and much larger areas may be necessary in the case of major commercial fisheries. The current no-take areas in URT may be too small to be effective.

The Social Dimension of Fishery Management in URT.

A system of fisheries management areas would be appropriate if the main objective is to contribute to sustainable livelihoods, but given the close overlap with biodiversity priorities, this would need careful planning. This is particularly important since the areas with highest fishing effort also overlap closely with those areas important for biodiversity such as Mtwara, Mafia, and Tanga. A 2001 survey resulted in an estimate of 20 000 full time fishermen on the mainland and a 2003 survey for Zanzibar indicated 18 000 fishermen (8 000 on Pemba and 10 000 on Unguja). The vast majority are artisanal and subsistence fishermen using unmechanized vessels in inshore shallow waters, rarely in more than 30 m depth. With a variety of gear, a wide range of species are taken including fish and invertebrates such as lobsters, prawns and mollusks. Invertebrates are also simply gathered on the tidal flats. This high dependency on fisheries can be partially attributed to the relatively poor soil conditions in coastal URT. Much of the coast is limestone and is suitable for agriculture only in periods of high rainfall. While there are fertile alluvial soils in deltaic areas, agriculture is limited to dry seasons because of flooding.

Many fishermen in URT fish far from their homes and often move in particular patterns along the coastline. Dago fishing, whereby fishermen travel long distances to fish, camping overnight often for several weeks, is a particular characteristic of the artisanal fishery in URT. It is generally related to the seasonally reversing monsoon winds that favor certain places at certain times of year, and to the need to find markets for their catch. Fishermen from Kojani, off the north coast of Pemba, may travel up to Kenya or as far south as Mozambique; others travel shorter distances, such as those from Mtwara who go up to Mafia, and those in northern Unguja who go down to southern Unguja (Menai Bay). The ratio of migratory fishermen to resident fishermen is not known, but even if it is small, it potentially makes community-based and/or area-based fisheries management difficult since dago fishermen are unlikely to be interested in local area management initiatives. The seasonal increase in fishing effort due to the arrival of dago fishermen can cause conflict with local communities. The presence of dago fishermen only accentuates the difficulty of enforcing MPAs and management areas.

Fisheries in URT are traditionally open-access (free entry) and thus the establishment of any form of fishery management area requires careful planning and extensive consultation with resident fishermen, as well as consideration of the impact on migratory fishermen. In several instances, the establishment of MPAs in URT have generated conflict with fishermen who were displaced or who were forced to reduce their effort. Although it is widely recommended by scientists and the international community that at least 20 percent of every marine ecosystem should be closed to fishing if marine biodiversity is to be adequately protected and fish stocks recovered, such measures require very careful consideration and can not be implemented in isolation. Cessation of damaging fishing methods such as dynamiting and beach seine netting may have as positive an impact on marine resources as would the imposition of MPAs, and in parts of URT this in fact seems to be the case. The collaborative management areas being established in the three northern districts might be the most appropriate approach. There, the management areas were defined and the regulations for their use are instigated and monitored by the fishermen themselves. The role that multiple-use marine parks (on mainland Tanzania) and community-managed conservation areas (such as Misali and Menai Bay on Zanzibar) might play has yet to be determined, but could be significant.

Prawn fishery. A system oriented towards fisheries management must also consider the prawn fishery on the mainland; it comprises both artisanal village fishers and a commercial fleet of some 24 trawlers. Both use the same areas: the Bagamoyo/Saadani area, the Kisiju area, and the Rufiji Delta. The Fisheries Department requires commercial boats to rotate around managed zones. But there is currently much conflict in the prawn fishery between trawlers whose activities damage the seabed, and artisanal fishermen using the same areas. There is thus an urgent need to develop a more effective management system for the prawn zones: one that gives greater protection to the prawn stock in river mouths and recognizes the needs of local fishing communities.

Pelagic fishery. Pelagic waters are considered to be fairly rich fishing grounds, but are less productive than some other areas in the WIO because URT waters are on the edge of the Indian Ocean gyre and thus do not benefit from upwellings. They are exploited for the large migratory pelagic species such as tuna that are taken by the few licensed commercial boats, and the presumed much larger number of illegal, unlicensed boats from foreign countries. The EU-supported regional fisheries project has provided the means for patrolling the waters using aerial surveys. Since this has been in place the number of boats requesting licenses has increased. To date, however, no effort has been made to manage the entire EEZ, or to establish no-take areas. Most management efforts focus on the territorial seas or to a small portion thereof corresponding to the 18 000 km² of continental shelf.

Eight Networks – Seven Core Priorities and the EEZ

URT faces a host of objectives that it can pursue to varying degrees. They include biodiversity conservation, protection of rare and threatened species, maintenance of region-wide ecosystem functions, fisheries management, recreation, education, research, and environmental aesthetics. The breadth of this list calls for a comprehensive system of marine and coastal resource management and protection characterized by a series of eight networks linked together at different levels. Through such an integrated system these objectives can be

addressed in a more coordinated and complementary fashion.

URT already has some components of a system of marine management but they are being implemented as independent units. They reflect some of the key marine biodiversity sites but they were not established with any overall plan in mind and therefore do not operate as a system. An effective system addresses the physical connections between sites, such as currents or migrating species, as well as institutional and managerial arrangements. It does not however imply that there should be a single management authority; an effective system can comprise a range of types of management areas, under different governance regimes adapted to local conditions.

Given the importance of biodiversity for URT, and the urgent need to meet socio-economic needs, the preferred option is one involving a range of different types of MPAs and MMAs. Such a mixed network takes advantage of existing management regimes and institutional arrangements, some of which are showing preliminary signs of success. For example, there are indications that collaborative fishery management areas as practiced in the northern mainland districts could be replicated elsewhere. Similarly, the designation and management of all mangrove forests as Reserves for sustainable use by local communities appears to have had a positive impact. Both the multiple use MPAs and the smaller sanctuary areas, managed in partnership with communities and/or the private sector, hold potential.

Blueprint 2050 shows seven core sub-national MPA/MMA networks in priority areas (Figure 1.1), complemented by sound management of the entire EEZ as an eighth network. The seven Core Priority Areas have already been recognized as priorities for biodiversity conservation (under the EAME reconnaissance [Box p 37]) and form a sound basis for an initial national system. Each of the seven core sub-national networks is larger than most MPAs, and each complex provides ecologically critical habitat; the areas are rich in benthic and/or pelagic features, marine species aggregations, or are characterized by high biomass and productivity. They encompass complexes that are particularly vulnerable or unique to the whole region – such as sites of high coral diversity or areas of endemism. Priorities are areas that are also threatened and vulnerable to disturbance or change from human induced or natural causes but still hold an opportunity for conservation. They serve as nodes for conservation that benefit the greater region; they focus regional attention, and provide linkages for conservation between the regional and local levels.

The proposed system is characterized by the following elements:

- Presence of *fully protected MPAs* or zones (or no-extraction areas) within each core network. These include actual MPAs such as the Chumbe Island Coral Sanctuary, and core areas within multiple use MPAs such as the fully protected zones within Mafia Island Marine Park.

- Inclusion of *multiple-use MPAs and MMAs* including fishery management areas, such as Mafia, Mnazi Bay, and Menai Bay. These sites can be considered crucial to the functioning of the marine and coastal environment on the whole, but may also be unique in themselves or provide habitat for unique species. These sites ideally include spawning aggregation areas, breeding or feeding grounds for key species; and areas that support the functioning of other habitats – coral reefs that help protect adjacent sandy beaches or rocky coasts from wave action, or estuaries that provide nutrients to offshore sites and purify water from land-based sources.

- Linkages to *transboundary MPAs and managed fishing areas.* There are important marine biodiversity areas on both of URT's coastal national boundaries – in the north with Kenya and in the south with Mozambique. Initiatives are underway at both sites to develop joint and/or integrated management activities.

At the national scale, the system would integrate all of these elements and link them with the broader ICM program that also in effect covers the entire EEZ. The MPAs and MMAs would ensure the protection of representative samples of marine biodiversity and of key areas for sustainable resource use. The ICM program would provide the mechanisms for protecting and managing the corridors and connectivity between them.

Photo Paavo Eliste

The Role of Science

It is worth noting here that, as in most countries, certain areas of the coast have been better studied than others because of their accessibility, scientific or economic interest, or other historical incident. Some sites considered as high biodiversity areas could simply be artifacts of greater research investment. This underlines the important role of science in future management decisions.

The lack of information on the ecology of the marine and coastal environment of URT, and of the areas most critical for maintaining ecosystems processes, remains a challenge to implementing an MPA/MMA system. In the near-term, a priority is to collate relevant information that is currently lodged with a range of government agencies, academic institutions, NGOs, and projects; and to ensure that there is some means of sharing and using it for the benefit of all. Hence mechanisms for cooperation between institutions are urgently required. A key long-term need is for targeted research on marine and coastal ecosystems to obtain a better understanding of ecological issues. Institutions such as IMS can play an important role in this, by developing close working relationships with existing MPAs and marine management areas and identifying their needs in terms of data and understanding of ecological processes.

Nevertheless, the precautionary approach dictates that knowledge gaps and limited capacity should not deter URT from developing an integrated marine and coastal zone management system. The basic elements for such a system are already in place. Moreover, even with the lack of scientific certainty as to the location, size, and number of managed or protected areas, an adaptive system will permit the incorporation of new scientific findings.

Ecological Endpoint

In 2004 Tanzania and Zanzibar have 10 designated MPAs. Many more are on the drawing boards. Coral reefs tend to be over-represented. Transboundary conservation initiatives are acknowledged as being important but are not yet formally recognized. There are management models in place that are state-of-the-art; at the local level, co-management is providing positive ecological impacts. In brief, there are simple systems in place that work. These are an important building block for what lies ahead.

Under Blueprint 2050, we foresee that all of the EEZ will be under some form of rational management that complements conservation and management efforts in the seven high priority core networks. About 14 500 km^2 of marine areas will fall under some form of management within these priority areas; this represents some 40 percent of the territorial seas around Tanzania and Zanzibar. Under this scenario, the managed areas would include most of the country's coral reefs, mangroves, wetlands, and important bird areas.

Getting there from here will require an approach that stresses learning and adaptation. At present, we know next to nothing about 99 percent of the marine areas within Tanzania's EEZ and coastal waters. It would be pure hubris to presume that we have all of the information we need to design a system that captures all of the ecological imperatives and will last for fifty years. Blueprint 2050 is thus as much a process as it is a template. The process relies on knowledge management and generation of the best available information for decision-making. If we acknowledge that we are not designing the system but, rather, are partners in its evolution, then the emergence of a complex system that works, from simple systems that work, will be inevitable.

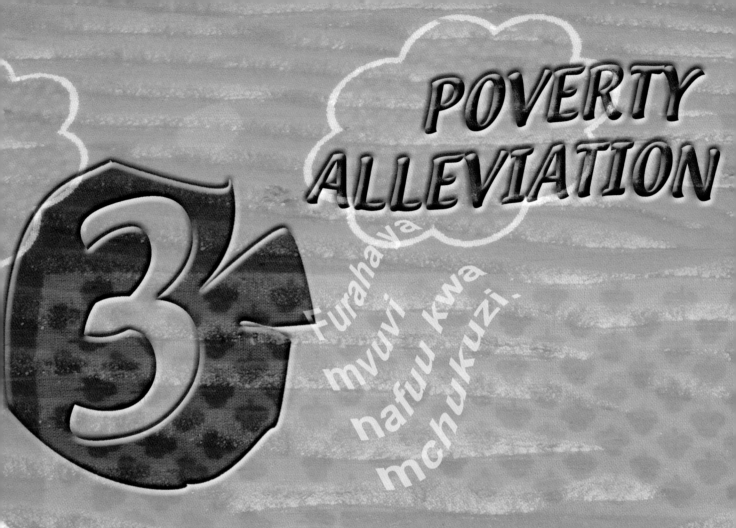

POVERTY ALLEVIATION

3

Furahaya mvuvi nafuu kwa mchukuzi.

We will spare no effort to free our fellow men, women and children from the abject and dehumanizing conditions of poverty, to which more than a billion of them are currently subjected.

UN Millennium Declaration – September 2000

Introduction

The Millennium Development Goal (MDG) for sub-Saharan Africa was to reduce poverty from levels of 47 percent in 1990 to about 24 percent of the population in 2015. An intermediate goal of 30 percent was established for 2005, implying that – in Tanzania – fewer than 10 million would be living on less than a poverty cut-off line of US$1 a day. Unfortunately, that goal has remained elusive. In 2004, while overall poverty levels are indeed about 30 percent, rural poverty levels in Tanzania are of the order of 50 percent. Eradicating poverty and achieving the MDG targets will require Herculean efforts.

The reasons for slow progress in poverty alleviation in rural areas to date are manifold, and it is not our intent to revisit or analyze the factors that have contributed to the successes or failures of past efforts. We do, however, note that the relationships between poverty and environmental degradation are more complex than were previously imagined. Traditional thinking often argued that, in some cases, poverty was a direct result of environmental degradation. In other cases, environmental degradation was a direct consequence of poverty. We now know much better that such models are over-simplified at best, flawed at worst. The interactions are much more complex, with external factors often exacerbating both poverty and environmental degradation. Recent work in Tanzania on poverty-environment linkages has shed new light on the complexity of these linkages.

Their findings suggest that poverty is strongly tied to the lack of secure access to resources; and that secure access is more readily disrupted in situations of environmental vulnerability. When ecosystems are poorly managed and are at their limits, it is more likely that feedback cycles contribute both to resource degradation and to poverty. The declining fish stocks in the Tanga region were an example of this. The feedback loops that reinforced both poverty and environmental degradation needed to be broken through some completely different model. In the case of Tanga, that model saw the emergence of adaptive co-management (ACM) approaches that involved considerable community effort to change the downward spiral. The ACM models stressed the development of alternative income generating activities (AIGAs) and, perhaps more significantly, saw an empowerment of local communities that involved them directly in local resource management decisions. The consequences of any mistakes would be borne by local populations. But benefits would also accrue to them if the right decisions were made. As a consequence, incentive structures changed dramatically and, today, both incomes and fish stocks are again on the rise. Tanga is a case in point for the application of best practices, in the interest of poverty alleviation and sustainable use. It is, in effect, a relatively simple model; the principles under which it was implemented can serve as a basis for replication elsewhere.

The principles are simple:

- The first principle is: *recognize impoverishment when it happens and resolve to do something about it.* While this may seem self-evident, complicity often prevents real progress from happening. The first part of this chapter thus considers the indicators of poverty, and provides snapshots of current conditions and what to look for; it also considers what roles MPAs have played to date in poverty alleviation.

- The second principle is: *focus proactively on increasing real incomes through alternative income generating activities.* Again, this may seem self-evident but what is less obvious is that these activities need not be large and glamorous get-rich-quick schemes. The most successful tend to involve simple replicable models that use technologies and methods appropriate to local economic and cultural conditions. They are often small scale in nature. The successful ones are often benign to the environment or are based on value added from the sustainable use of existing resources. Typically they involve speedy returns on modest investments, with collaboration among small groups of individuals. Investments in seaweed farming are a case in point. The second part of this chapter tells a broader story of AIGAs, and how they can be used to address vulnerability.

- The third principle is: *decentralize responsibility to permit meaningful adaptive co-management.* This implies that local populations are strongly involved in resource management. It means that they have scope to experiment, make mistakes, realize successes, learn, and adapt. This adaptive capacity is incredibly important for long-term well-being, as the adaptive mechanisms that are developed through such experimentation will be the same ones that protect these people from future shocks, thus reducing their vulnerability. The third part of this chapter thus looks more closely at some of the cases of adaptive co-management, drawing lessons for replication elsewhere.

Photo Paavo Eliste

Managing Perceptions – A Sociologist Speaks

Poverty alleviation is often regarded as a broad goal, but we must not forget that poverty itself is an intensely personal phenomenon. Broad definitions of poverty are important, income generation is important, and sharing in decision-making and management is important. But all of these ideas have implications at a very individual level. Before looking at the broader picture, we must therefore recognize that the perceptions of individuals can be equally important, and they may differ from what we expect. Let us take a few moments for some professional insights – from our resident sociologist – into how perceptions can influence poverty.

Why are perceptions important to an understanding of poverty?

An individual's perceptions often have a great impact on their behavior (and their sense of well-being). The behavior may be quite different from what we expect just by looking, as outsiders, at their situation or circumstances.

You imply that the perceptions and the facts or reality may thus be quite different?

Yes, in a sense. But the perceptions are just as much of a reality as all the other influences around them. To the extent that perceptions influence behavior, we must treat them seriously, even if they appear to contradict factual evidence. Some group that feels unjustly treated, for example, can become a powerful political influence.

Why might perceptions and reality differ?

More often than not it is because we, as outsiders, tend to look at *absolute* conditions, while individuals often consider *relative* positions. Someone making $2 a day in the midst of a community where everybody else makes $3 a day is likely to perceive themselves as more impoverished than if they were in the midst of others that were making $1 a day. But our external assessment may consider that person better off in the wealthier community – because there is more potential for sharing – than in the poorer community.

So the perception of one's position compared to that of others is important. But perceptions seem to change quite frequently in response to external factors. Why does that happen?

In such cases, there is also a change in the relative positions, but it occurs because of "before and after" circumstances. An individual might say, "before the MPA was established, I could fish whenever I wanted with anything I wanted to use. Now, I can only fish at certain times, using certain equipment. I have worse access and am less well off." But our observations might show that the person is making more money, because fish are bigger and are easier to catch, and there is less waste.

Well it seems to me that you are both right in that case. Access has indeed gone down, but maybe the fisher is better off.

Perhaps. But the point about "perceptions" is that the fisher might not see it that way. He will acknowledge that the fish are bigger, and that he is richer, but he would then go on to claim that he would be richer still if he could have the same access he enjoyed previously. So he gets annoyed, and he may try to break the rules to get more of the bigger fish. His perceptions thus become a real enforcement problem.

But if he is in a minority, it might not matter?

Even if he is just among a minority with such perceptions, the situation can become a real management challenge. Enforcement costs increase, conflict increases, if left unchecked others may follow that individual's example and within a short time the area may again be over-fished. So the perceptions need to be treated seriously.

What is the best way to deal with such perceptions?

Contrary to what I may have implied, enforcement is a last recourse. Before it ever gets to the point where the perceptions lead to delinquent behavior, we need to provide means to manage the perceptions. This implies foremost that we need to know what the perceptions are, and then provide ways for people to express themselves and resolve any problems. Adaptive co-management mechanisms provide such processes. Social pressure and traditional outlets for expression that emerge during ACM processes are an important part of problem recognition and resolution. In Tanga, for example, one would not claim that – at the outset – everybody had the same idea of fishery management. Over time, however, perceptions have changed and people feel more fairly treated than they might have felt at the outset.

Has anybody ever looked critically at the perceptions in coastal communities in Tanzania?

Yes, we did. Surveys made during 2003 looked at some 24 villages in coastal Tanzania. These were at six sites: Tanga, Mafia Island, Menai Bay, Jozani-Chwaka Bay, Misali Island and Kilwa. A total of 749 households were involved, capturing just over 4000 individuals. Surveys were made to look at the usual demographic and income variables, as well as the wealth of individuals in terms of their assets and liabilities. Most of that type of information is readily quantified and gives us good snapshots of what conditions are like generally. But then we went a step further, and asked people more specifically about their various perceptions.

If perceptions cannot be readily quantified, how do you capture them?

The methods used are not at all complicated. In fact, they are so familiar that everybody uses them in their day-to-day interactions with friends and acquaintances. We simply sit down with people – just as you might in casual conversation with friends – and ask them what they think about something, or what their experience has been. This type of "open-ended" format is then later formalized by classifying their responses into various categories; with a large number of respondents, usually just a handful of different types of responses and patterns emerge. We can analyze those patterns.

What were the types of questions you asked?

We asked people their perceptions on a number of items. Of village leaders, we asked: "What do you think are the most important problems in your village?" On this account, 25 percent cited the lack of clean water. We asked these same leaders what they thought were the most significant causes of poverty locally. Some 22 percent thought that it was connected to poor fishing gear, while only 5 percent attributed it to a lack of technical support or knowledge.

Similar questions of perception were asked of individual households. About 80 percent of the households thought their food situation had become worse or remained unchanged over the prior five years.

Did people have strong opinions on MPAs?

These were perhaps the most interesting. The villages chosen were selected because there had been some exposure to MPAs. All of the areas with the exception of Kilwa had an existing MPA close by. We asked a very specific question of these individuals: "What do you dislike about MPAs?" Fortunately, 23 percent had no dislikes at all. Some 10 percent had non-specific complaints. But of those with some specific complaints, the most significant complaint was associated with the limited or reduced access to their fishery or related resources. These complaints alone outnumbered all other complaints put together (those associated with harassment by marine authority, lack of community participation, lack of transparency in what was being done).

What do you deduce from this perception?

To interpret this, we first need to understand that the concept of "access" is an important one in all modern definitions of poverty. Whereas we used to think of poverty just in terms of income, we now regard access to education, healthcare, employment opportunities, credit, or natural resources as a fundamental component of poverty measures. The lack of access contributes substantially to greater poverty. The fact that 35 percent of all complaints associated with MPAs were associated with a perception of reduced access is definitely of concern. It is thus a situation that warrants close monitoring because, if left unchecked, it can lead to management difficulties for MPAs.

Recognizing Impoverishment – Are Coastal Populations the Poorest of the Poor?

Photo Paavo Eliste

As noted by our resident sociologist, there is no single measure of poverty. Income has been classically used, but we now recognize that poverty is many-faceted and that no single indicator can capture all of its dimensions. We therefore start here by taking a look at typical conditions in coastal villages. Where household results are given, the results rely on the same sample as that described above.

Poverty Measures

Poverty along the coastal regions of Tanzania is widespread; on average, 85 percent of the sample population survives on less than a dollar per person per day. The average monthly per capita consumption expenditures in 2003 for the sample population was about US$21 for both mainland Tanzania and Zanzibar. This is roughly two-thirds of the established poverty line of US$30.

Three poverty indices are presented in Table 3.1. While these three poverty indicators do not show a significant variation across regions, some important

observations can be made. The poverty gap and the poverty severity index, for example, show that the poor in Kilwa seem relatively worse off compared to the poor in the other mainland regions. Similarly, the poor in Unguja appear somewhat worse off than the poor in Pemba. Such widespread poverty is an indication of the pressing need for undertaking poverty alleviation initiatives in these regions.

Access to Services

Living standards are also determined by access to social services and infrastructure (Table 3.2). In coastal Tanzania, limited access is generally a hindrance to expanding household economic

Table 3.1   Poverty measures in Tanzania coastal villages

Indicator	Mainland			Zanzibar	
	Tanga	Mafia	Kilwa	Unguja	Pemba
Household consumption (US$/mo)	21.25	21.15	19.53	20.04	20.69
Poverty headcount	84	86	86	86	82
Poverty gap index	36	39	41	39	34
Poverty severity index	19	21	23	22	19

The "poverty headcount" measures the percentage of people living below the poverty line. The "poverty gap" is an index of how poorly off these poor are; it gives a measure of the depth of the income deficit (the level below the poverty line) among the poor. The third measure – "poverty severity" – provides an additional distributional element by showing the depth of poverty amongst the poorest individuals among the poor. In all cases, the higher the value of the poverty measure, the greater the level of impoverishment.

Source: Village survey, 2003.

Table 3.2 Distance to social services and infrastructure

Destination	Mainland			Zanzibar	
	Tanga	Mafia	Kilwa	Unguja	Pemba
Market	1.7	6.8	47.7	75.0	36.3
Bus Station	50.2	17.8	93.7	3.2	21.9
Primary School	45.0	7.3	26.0	17.9	39.8
Health Facility	56.2	76.4	7.8	20.5	39.8
Hospital	547.5	265.7	702.0	120.2	69.5
Firewood source	75.0	36.3	30.0	66.7	141.2
Water source (dry season)	5.0	9.6	25.1	8.8	18.5

This shows the relative isolation of villages, as measured by the average time it takes (in minutes) to get to key services.

opportunities. The villages included in the survey are located in rural areas where, in all but two of the villages, roads are constructed of dirt and are in poor or very poor condition.

Savings and Credit

Access to credit and the role of savings is often a useful indicator of the depth of poverty. First, the availability of savings or access to credit in itself demonstrates that there is some income available to generate such wealth or service debt. Second, the savings themselves provide an opportunity for reducing vulnerability in times of hardship. Moreover, the existence of savings or willingness to borrow establishes a cultural precedent that is not always evident in rural settings; forest communities in Tanzania's interior, for example, show a high savings ethic.

In Tanzania's coastal communities, evidence suggests that savings rates – although low – are above the rural norm for the country. In our coastal household sample, most households store their surplus earnings inside the house or use it to buy food. Of the surveyed households, 13 percent reported having a savings account in a bank, and 17 percent said they participated in an informal credit and savings group. While this is a much higher rate than in rural Tanzania, where the corresponding figures are around 4 percent and 3 percent respectively, the norm is still not to set aside cash.

Savings can also occur through retaining the physical asset rather than keeping money in a bank. For example, women engaged in seaweed culture may postpone selling some of the crop until they need money. Other women buy *khangas/lesos*, which they can give (in case they do not have money) for weddings, funerals or newborns.

In the same coastal areas, credit access is very poor. The majority of households have never borrowed and when they do, they usually go to relatives. Only 3 percent of households have borrowed from a credit and savings scheme, and of those, over half said it was somewhat or very difficult to repay the loans. In some cases women keep their money in micro credit revolving funds (*upatus*) where they are able to earn a lump sum that they tend to spend on social activities. In all villages interviewed, *upatu* credit and savings systems were identified as one of the women's most strategic means of coping with income insecurity.

Evidence suggests that saving and credit access are not a normal part of community life, but that their introduction is possible. There was neither credit nor savings in Mafia until a micro credit and savings scheme was established as part of the activities of the Mafia Island Marine Park project. Saving and Credit Committees have been formed in 9 of 11 villages in the Park. After 3 months of deposit, and to a maximum of US$1 000, a member can borrow up to twice as much as his deposited amount at an annual interest rate of 12 percent. Anyone who receives an interest free loan from the project – for beekeeping, fishing gear replacement, or a small shop – must become a member of the Savings and Credit Society. Without the Savings and Credit Society, saving money in practice is very difficult here. Setting money aside is normally impossible.

At the Jozani-Chwaka Bay Conservation Area, a Grameen model savings and credit scheme was established in 1999 for the purpose of issuing loans to village groups to be used for developing small enterprises. A total of 76 groups were formed. It proved difficult to identify income-generating activities so loans were used for purposes other than small investments, and loans that were used for investment purposes were too small to successfully establish enterprises. The end result was, of course, a low repayment rate. The Grameen model was subsequently replaced with an Accumulated Savings and Credit Association (ASCA). Through the ASCA, individuals can borrow up to three times the amount saved but must repay in three months with 5 percent interest. Training on how to manage the Association, and on alternative income generation, was also provided.

At Misali Island Marine Conservation Area, by June 2003, a total of 389 persons (189 women and 200 men) from 8 villages had obtained loans through the credit and savings scheme. The scheme follows the same design that was established in the Jozani-Chwaka Bay Conservation Area project. It provides loans for supplemental livelihood projects such as beekeeping, seaweed farming, vegetable gardens, and mushroom growing. Everyone with loans is required to take part in organized training on how to form a community-based organization, how to save, and how to plan and manage small-scale income-generating projects.

Poverty and MPAs

The above examples relating to savings and credit demonstrate that there are some potential positive impacts of MPAs in the general structure of economic behavior. But can one make any generalizations about the impact of MPAs on poverty?

Assessing the impact of MPAs or other resource management policies on coastal communities is important to ensure their long-term sustainability. The poorest of fishermen, those that do not have access to a boat or have only small boats, generally fish in near-shore waters. These fishermen would be disproportionately affected by coastal developments (including tourism) or MPA policies that restrict their access to these areas.

To evaluate the impact of MPAs on poverty in the coastal communities of Tanzania, we compared the poverty rates of villages in or near MPAs, to those of villages outside of MPAs. Table 3.3 shows that poverty rates among fishing households do not differ between these two groups. Partly this is because these particular MPAs have been only recently established. It often takes a long time before the impacts of establishing an MPA translate into significant improvements in household incomes. Also, conservation efforts by an MPA also benefit outside fishing grounds and those villages who frequent them. Hence, villages in the surrounding areas, outside the MPA, will also realize increases in fish catch and household incomes; thus rendering difficult a comparison of villages inside and those outside MPAs. Just looking at relative poverty rates therefore does not allow us to draw

Table 3.3 Poverty headcounts by household main activity in Tanzania coastal communities

Activity	Full Sample	MPA	Non-MPA	Mainland	Zanzibar
Fishing	83*	85	83	86*	81*
Farming	88*	90	85	87	89
Employment	78*	73*	93*	62*	85*
Trade	82	88	71	82	81
Total	85	86	83	85	84

This shows the percentage of households living below the poverty line, as a function of their primary source of household income and whether their village is near an MPA or not, or whether on the mainland or Zanzibar.

"*" shows statistically different at 5 percent level.

definite conclusions about the welfare of this group, or to what extent the poorest within this group were affected by the establishment of MPAs. On the other hand, the results also show that the MPAs have no immediate negative impact on the communities. This is an important result because it is often presumed that *negative* impacts are more immediate given that MPAs are often associated with restricted access.

The establishment of MPAs does appear to have an impact on poverty rates among those households that can benefit from the alternative employment opportunities generated. This is an encouraging result because other studies have found that promoting income-generating businesses as part of community-based coastal management improves community interest and participation and, therefore, the likelihood of success. The proportion of households employed in non-fishing or non-farming activities was typically two to three times higher for MPA villages than for non-MPA villages.

Using AIGAs to Improve Incomes and Reduce Vulnerability

The challenge for alleviating poverty is to improve access to services and generate greater incomes without inflicting negative impacts on the resource base. In this section we look at the current picture, and then consider three different case studies on how AIGAs might improve circumstances. These are: (i) expanding incomes using existing techniques (mariculture development in the nearshore); (ii) expanding incomes through new areas of interest (cultural tourism); and, (iii) reducing income vulnerability through methods that enhance the environment and improve incomes (brushwood parks).

Current Picture

Most households surveyed depend on natural resources for their livelihood, deriving their income primarily from farming or fishing activities. It is interesting, therefore, to check whether poverty rates across households vary systematically according to the income generating activity in which the household is primarily engaged. Table 3.3 shows that there are significant differences in poverty rates by households' main activity. Households reporting fishing as the main income generating activity in the mainland coastal regions of Tanzania are significantly poorer than fishing households in Zanzibar. Also, households involved in non-resource based employment activities are significantly better off if they are near an MPA.

We also investigated the main economic activities by gender of the head of household. While fishing was slightly more common than farming as the main activity of male-headed households, most female-headed households practiced farming as their main economic activity. Agriculture was also important for female spouses (not heads of household) who worked outside the house, with 65 percent of them declaring farming as their main economic activity, followed by fishing (15 percent) and petty trading (10 percent).

Poverty rates across farming households are the highest. But the proportion of households declaring farming as their main income generating activity declines as household income increases in both mainland Tanzania and Zanzibar. Trends for fishing between mainland Tanzania and Zanzibar, however, are different. In Zanzibar, there is a significant increase in the share of households engaged in fishing as household income rises. This may be partly due to the scarcity of land in Zanzibar. With less flexibility of substitution into alternative livelihood activities, fishing becomes relatively more important.

AIGAs and Existing Activities – The Case for Mariculture

The most obvious choice for alternative income generation is simply to improve existing methods through expansion or simple modifications to ensure responsible resource management. The survey work showed that while fishing is a core activity, there are numerous other activities occurring in coastal villages on which one can build. We take a closer look here at the role of seaweed farming.

Different types of fishing, seaweed farming, and various types of agriculture dominate the range of resource-based productive activities in which households are engaged (Table 3.4). A greater proportion of female-headed households was engaged in algae farming, particularly of *Eucheuma spinosum* (26.2 percent of female-headed households versus 15.2 percent of male-headed ones). Seaweed farming was most frequent in the Jozani-Chwaka Bay and Menai Bay areas on Unguja, while on the mainland its greatest incidence was in parts of Mafia and Kilwa (Figure 3.1).

Returns from such activities can be quite favorable, although they are subject to fluctuations in international market conditions. Tanzania is currently one of a handful of countries that produces seaweed for international export: total cultivated production world-wide in 2003 was approximately 1 100 000 mt, of which over 90 percent was produced in East and Southeast Asia. Tanzania's production of about 7 000 mt thus represents only a small share in a large market. *Eucheuma* species represent less than 3 percent of international production, and are the major export species for

Table 3.4 Resource-based household subsistence and employment activities

Activity	Households Engaged in Activity	Percent (of 749 households)
• *Marine fauna*		
Fish	355	47.4
Crustaceans	117	15.6
Sea cucumbers	32	4.3
Mollusks	18	2.4
Other	3	0.4
• *Seaweed farming*		
E. spinosum	125	16.7
E. cottonii	69	9.2
• *Mangrove extraction*	25	3.3
• *Coral mining*	7	0.9
• *Salt mining*	3	0.4
• *Sand mining*	6	0.8
• *Farming – Crops*		
Cassava	375	50.1
Bananas	245	32.7
Rice	206	27.5
Maize	141	18.8
Millet	117	15.6
Sweet potatoes	107	14.3
Groundnuts	7	0.9
Tomatoes	32	4.3
Pineapples	11	1.5
Pulses	41	5.5
Simsim (oil seed)	10	1.3
Other	4	0.5
• *Farming – Agroforestry*		
Coconuts	110	14.7
Cashew nuts	41	5.5
Mangoes	30	4.0
Cloves	15	2.0
Citrus	2	0.3
Other	33	4.4
• *Livestock keeping*		
Cattle	38	5.1
Goats/sheep	15	2.0
Poultry	90	12.0
Donkey/horse	1	0.1
Other	3	0.4

Figure 3.1   Frequency of seaweed farming in Tanzania coastal villages

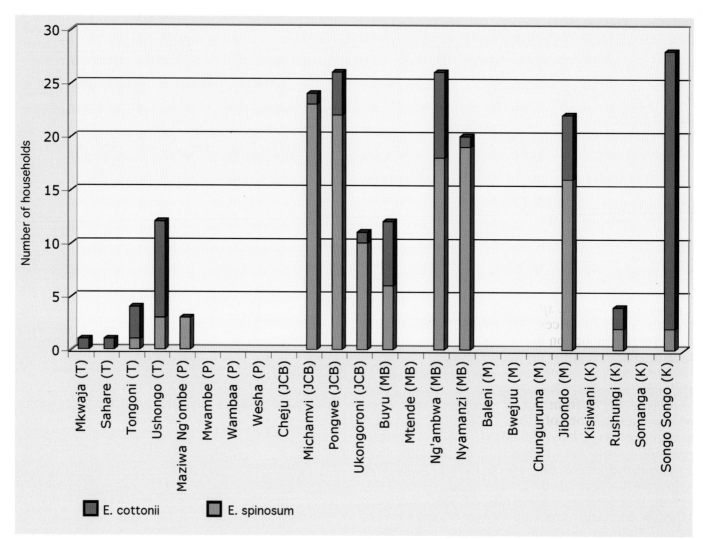

This shows the number of households engaged in seaweed farming across six sites, with four villages surveyed in each of the following areas: Tanga (T), Pemba (P), Jozani-Chwaka Bay (JCB), Menai Bay (MB), Mafia (M) and Kilwa (K). Source: Based on coastal village survey, 2003.

Shipwrecks – An Underwater Cultural Heritage.

Shipwrecks abound in the coastal area. The majority of these sites have had no documentation or research conducted on them as yet and most have no name. These include a wreck near Misali Island; and another south of Panza Island. Zanzibar in particular is famous for the remains of numerous old ships in its territorial waters. It is believed that many Portuguese and Dutch ships sank off the Eastern Coast of Zanzibar en route to the Indian sub-continent during 16th and 17th centuries. The 1872 hurricane, which swept away almost all the clove trees and coconut palms in Zanzibar, is believed to have sunk between 70 – 100 ships and dhows that were anchored in Zanzibar harbors. Remains of the British warship Pegasus, sunken by German guns during World War I, still lie in Zanzibar harbor, and it is a popular diving site, as is the Great Northener shipwreck of 1900. Records indicate that several ships and dhows were also sunken in various spots during the suppression of the slave trade. Recently some research was conducted jointly by the Department of Archives, Museums and Antiquities in Zanzibar, and a marine archaeology company based in Mauritius. Three more ships were located in Zanzibar's waters through this research, two of which were iron ships thought to be from London and Hyderabad and to have sunk in the 1860-1870 period. The third was a wooden ship sunken c. 1845, probably of French origin in which was found cutlery, old glasses, bottles, cups, and bowls.

Tanzania. While *E. spinosum* production levels are strong, 2004 prices are currently quite weak. *E. cottonii* production has been characterized by greater price stability but production systems are more erratic and experimentation with this variety still needs further development. In recent years, however, yields from seaweed were adequate to provide net incomes of the order of US$10/day per participating member.

AIGAs and New Activities – The Case for Cultural Tourism

Many of the visitors to Zanzibar enjoy not only the natural environment, but also the historical and cultural significance of the buildings, monuments, and other artifacts. As a centre of trade in the Western Indian Ocean for centuries, the traditional ways of Zanzibar are regarded by many a visitor as a highlight of their overall experience. Cultural tourism is important in many countries, and cultural aspects even feature as part of the IUCN definition of MPAs. AIGAs based on the sustainable use of this cultural heritage provide a duel opportunity for alleviating poverty and protecting or restoring cultural resources.

Opportunities for cultural tourism abound in coastal areas. The Tanzanian coast and islands is particularly rich in cultural heritage resources; the physical evidence of a long history of settlement, including periods of notable wealth, stretches back to at least 800AD. The area is scattered with monuments of the Swahili civilization from the beginning of the 9th century (Figure 3.2).

On the mainland, The Antiquities Department, which falls under the Ministry of Natural Resources and Tourism (MNRT), is the governmental body assigned as custodian of the cultural heritage. While there are over 500 identified sites on the mainland, only 17 have offices, personnel and a budget for their upkeep. Along the coast these include: the Tongoni Ruins and Amboni Caves in Tanga region; Kaole Ruins and Bagamoyo historical town (the Caravanserai and the Old Fort) near Bagamoyo; and Kilwa Kisiwani and Songo Mnara in the Lindi region. Part of the Department's mission is to develop cultural tourism in a sustainable way.

On Zanzibar, there are 44 historical sites and monuments listed dating from the 9th to the 20th centuries; 21 are on Unguja, and 23 on Pemba. Most of the early sites and monuments are located along the coast of both islands. These figures exclude the buildings of Stone Town on Unguja, which is designated by UNESCO as a World Heritage Site. Livingstone House – a building with connections to the East African slave trade – is the current head office of Zanzibar's Department of Fisheries.

Figure 3.2   A 1966 plan of coastal sites of archaeological and historical interest

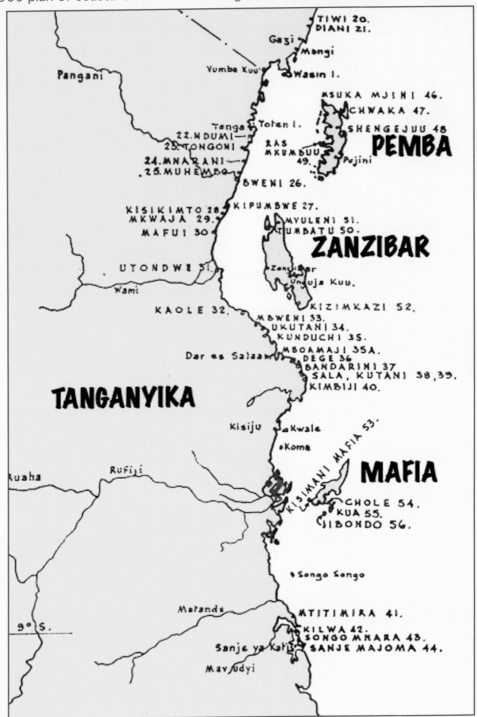

Plan by Peter S Garlake, The early Islamic architecture of the East African coast, p 123, copyright British Institute in East Africa, Nairobi, London. Published for the Institute by the Oxford University Press. Reproduced with permission of BIEA.

Both cultural and natural resources are valuable assets. Where these assets are sustainably utilized they can contribute significantly to development, and to improving livelihoods in impoverished areas. In many places these cultural and natural resources are adjacent to one another. At Kilwa, visitors must cross mangrove forests and sand beaches to view the monuments. Few visitors will fail to notice the scurrying crabs in the sand and other fascinating signs of seashore life. Some will pause for bird watching or stop to admire the majestic baobab trees.

With this abundance of both cultural and natural resources in such close proximity along the coastline and islands of Tanzania, there are significant potential benefits to local communities from a policy of shared planning and management. A good example is the Pangani Cultural Tourism Program which runs a training program to provide community-led tours for visitors. These include a visit to a former slave labor camp and slave market site; a river cruise through the coconut plantations; a walk through Pangani historical town; and a fishing experience with a local fisherman.

Training Pangani community members as guides has improved livelihoods and benefited local communities. Proceeds from activities are split between the guides themselves, the administrative cost of running a cultural tourism office, and a development project identified by the local community. The successful Cultural Tourism Program at Pangani could be extended or replicated elsewhere, also expanding on specific AIGAs related to the provision of tourist services.

AIGAs as a Way to Combat Vulnerability – The Case for Brushwood Parks

In 2003, Rufiji district was confronted with the lowest rainfall in 50 years. The Rufiji River, the largest in East Africa, usually overtops its banks in April, bringing life to hundreds of thousands of hectares of floodplain and a dozen flood-dependent lakes. In 2003 the mighty river was dormant in its dwindling dry-season bed. Worse still, famished lions left the neighboring Selous Game Reserve and went on a rampage in the floodplain, killing 28 farmers. Without crops to harvest, the local communities were forced to supplement their income from forestry, felling thousands of trees of slow-growing hardwood species for a pittance. It was a tough year for Rufiji.

But not all communities in the region faced disaster. The village of Mtanza-Msona, in the western floodplain, had been implementing a Village Environment Management Plan since 2001. As part of this on-going plan, they close Lake Mtanza, their main lake, to fisheries for 3 months each year. This creates a tranquil environment for the fish during spawning and early growth. Mr Moshi Makasamala, the village fish recorder, has shown that both catch per unit effort and the duration of the fishing season increases under this management regime. Before, the shallow lake would be fished out by July because both the adult spawners, trapped in the lake after the flood, and the young fish of the year would be harvested. Catches would be negligible until the next flood.

Still, the pressing need for livelihood alternatives during the closed season pushed the community to look into other solutions. A system of "brushwood parks", common in West Africa, was proposed for the lake by IUCN. According to the village elders, this fisheries management tool had existed locally of old and was known as *misakasaka*.

Preparations began in December 2002 when social, economic, technical and cultural aspects of the proposed trials were resolved through field visits and group discussions. It was thought that women, who do not in general share in the fishery resource, might be in a position to participate in the management of and returns from the brushwood parks. Three brushwood parks, one of 10 m and two of 20 m diameter, were constructed during the wet season. The branches used

misakasaka and are constructing new ones. The researchers are currently analyzing the data for feedback sessions with the villagers' decision-making forum. There are indications that the Tilapia-like *Oreochromis urolepis*, the species that contributed most to the cash profits, is breeding in the brushwood park but this needs to be confirmed. Much remains to be investigated on the life-cycle and habitat preference of the most lucrative species. Also, the potential of a non-fished *misakasaka*, managed as a permanent breeding site, needs to be evaluated and discussed with the community. If the analysis turns out favorably, expansion to the other floodplain lakes is a possibility. Increasingly, canoes and fishing gear are owned by traders who employ fishers. The intent is that brushwood parks will remain firmly in the hands of the local men and women.

for construction were carefully selected on the basis of durability, non-toxicity, and abundance. They were soaked first and construction itself took each group of 20 villagers about 3 hours. It is essential that these parks remain in place undisturbed for at least 4 months. This allows fish to settle and to reproduce and grow there, thus contributing to the lake's fisheries in general. If harvested sooner, the parks are essentially fish-aggregating devices and not the spawning and nursery habitat intended.

In July and August the three parks were harvested and yielded 1 800 kg of fish in total. For fishers, used to catches of 3 to 10 kg per day, the result was impressive. Dozens of men, women and children helped with the sorting and cleaning of over 30 000 fish and over half of those, especially the small catfish, were handed out free to all participants, a much appreciated protein supplement. Fish traders and smokers were forewarned of the harvest and the high value fish were turned into much needed cash on the same day. Baskets of fish were loaded on bicycles for sale in the neighboring villages. The rest went by bus to more distant markets. A story also traveled with the fish; the story told that, on the night of 19 August 2003, each household in Mtanza-Msona ate fish from a single catch.

The villagers have already evaluated the experience. They are recycling the branches of the previous

Developing Meaningful Adaptive Co-Management

All of the above examples showed differing degrees of co-management. Mariculture activities generally involve a few households with some private sector partners. Any development of cultural tourism will involve partnerships between the private sector, local communities, and government agencies responsible for protecting the country's cultural resources. The Brushwood Parks in Rufiji demonstrate co-management involving local community initiatives. All of these models are, in addition, what we would call "adaptive" to the extent that those responsible for the resource and the assets can learn directly from their experience in any given period, and thus modify their behavior accordingly in the next period. The Tanga Program of fisheries co-management is also a good example of ACM.

Excuse this brief interruption, but we have heard a lot about adaptive co-management. What is it, precisely?

To me it has a lot to do with deliberate experimentation. You start by managing something and then decide that maybe not all is going that well. You set a hypothesis, design a test for it, do the test, deduce your results, and adapt your management appropriately.

That is what we would call the adaptive part of management. It is common in scientific circles and, when applied properly, generally describes a learning cycle. But most scientists know that experiments themselves often generate results that answer questions not directly related to the hypothesis. You ask one question, do an experiment, then get an answer – but to a different question.

That's right. Serendipity and learning from accidents is as much a part of science as is deliberate investigation.

Exactly. And that is where the human learning element becomes so very important. Experiments are often sloppier than we would like them to be. But human systems are capable of using a diversity of information – even if it seems disconnected, randomly generated, or accidentally observed – to make better management decisions. This is all part of adaptation.

So far you have spoken about adaptive management, but my question also had to do with "co-management". What does the "co-" have to do with any of this?

All it means is that there is more than one player involved in the picture. Agreements are reached that share rights and responsibilities for enforcement, monitoring, cost-sharing, revenue-sharing, and so on.

Within Tanzania, a comprehensive example of ACM is that associated with the Tanga experience. It demonstrates the use of a few formalized instruments for sharing, and also shows how learning resulted in subsequent adaptation of management styles. The Tanga Program is acknowledged worldwide as a practical example of the application of effective methods for community-based coastal management. The core strategy of the program has been action planning—the use of issue-based plans, outlining specific actions targeted at either the causes or effects of problems, and providing detailed guidance on how they will be implemented, monitored, and adapted.

But that seems redundant. There is always more than one player involved in any form of resource management.

True, but it is seldom explicitly acknowledged. Local fishermen may feel they have no control. Or all regulations may be centrally administered and enforced. The point of "co-management" is that all parties agree on the divisions of responsibility.

Permit me to interrupt. I would add to that one more thing. The arrangements might themselves change. One thing we see in ecological systems is that the rules themselves seem to change. Fish gender is a nice example of that. Some reef fish species are born as one gender but undergo a gender change as ecological circumstances require. Also, successful behavioral strategies in one period may be unsuccessful in the next. In studies of birds, monogamy is at times the most successful long-term survival strategy when others are promiscuous, yet promiscuity can be most successful when others are monogamous. The dominant strategies therefore change with time and circumstances. These attributes are very common in complex systems and come about from the feedback loops inherent in such systems.

That's an excellent point. So ACM is a flexible approach to management that includes deliberate learning and experimentation, and a clear understanding of the division of responsibilities and rights among stakeholders. Most significantly, however, the system can also evolve such that this division of responsibilities will itself change as more experience is acquired over time.

The Tanga Coastal Zone Conservation and Development Program was initiated in 1994 to halt the decline of the economic wellbeing of coastal fishing villages in the Tanga region resulting from a decline of fish resources. This decline was attributed to over fishing and the intensive and long-term use of destructive fishing gears and methods. The Tanga Program was designed to improve coastal wellbeing by empowering local communities to restore and protect the coastal environment. The three coastal districts of the Tanga region have ecologically important and diverse marine habitats including coral reefs, mangrove forests, estuaries and bays, and sea grass beds. In total there are 96 fringing and patch reefs along the 180 km shore of the Tanga region.

Phase one of the Program (July 1994 – June 1997) had two objectives: to strengthen the capacity of local public institutions to undertake integrated coastal management, and to work with coastal communities to manage coral reefs and other natural resources. Phase two, which ended in December 2000, focused on the development and implementation of collaborative fisheries and reef management plans. Phase three has continued with a similar focus.

When the Tanga Program began a strategic decision was made to work at the most decentralized level (village, ward and district), rather than with regional governmental bodies, to develop institutional capacity and plans for coastal management. This proved to be an important decision and was consistent with policy changes in Tanzania, such as the Local Government Reform Act of 1998 and the Land Act of 1999.

Nine villages were selected (three in each district of Muheza, Tanga, and Pangani) to take part in a participatory resource assessment of coral reefs and coastal forests, and in an overall socio-economic assessment. These studies described ecosystem condition, resource use patterns and priority resource management issues. The Program intentionally invested much time and effort into the assessment process to ensure that the participants; i.e., the resource users and managers, were the ones to identify and prioritize issues and recommend actions. A number of priority resource management issues were selected: (i) over fishing and destructive fishing methods; (ii) poor government; (iii) lack of enforcement and management; (iv) coastal erosion; (v) destruction of mangroves; (vi) lack of firewood and building materials; (vii) poor agricultural production due to vermin; (viii) beach pollution; and, (ix) lack of basic sanitation in villages.

In July 1995, the three participating districts were invited to select one village each to begin a process of action planning directed at these issues. The three villages were selected to illustrate a range of different situations and challenges for coastal and marine management. The villages of Kigombe, Kipumbwi, and Mwambani were selected and with assistance from extension staff, village participants began to analyze the causes and consequences of problems, and to develop actions that could improve the situation. In the villages, a management committee was formed for each of the two to four resource issues that were identified as priorities. The Program provided training on how to formulate action plans with clear, achievable objectives, work plans, monitoring, and evaluation. The first action plans were one-year plans with evaluation and revision every six months. Later, they were structured with a three-month planning horizon. The first plans were formally adopted by the Village Committees and the District Advisory Committees in early 1996.

The second stage of action planning (1996-1999) was directed at marine ecosystem issues (such as reduced fish catch and dynamite fishing) shared across more than one village. Implementation of village specific action plans continued in the initial villages, and additional villages were added to two of the first three villages (Kigombe and Kipumbwi) to develop multi-village fisheries management plans.

As a response to the conflicts created by the attempt to do single-village management of coral reefs, the program decided that all villages that share a specific fishing area should be equal partners in developing, implementing, monitoring, and evaluating the fisheries management plan. A system was created in which each participating village elects a Village Environmental Committee responsible for developing a plan for fisheries management in their village. The village committees feed into a Central Coordinating Committee (CCC) comprised of representatives from all the villages taking part in the collaborative management scheme. The CCC is responsible for formulating a management plan approved by all villages. The collaborative fisheries management plans include actions, common rules, and penalties. The CCC is also responsible for resolving inter-village disputes and proposing bylaws to complement the implementation of the management plan. After the plan is approved by all villages and adopted by the CCC, the Village Environmental Committees are responsible for implementing village-based actions, while the CCC is responsible for overseeing overall plan implementation and monitoring. Currently, all 42 coastal villages in the Tanga region are to some extent involved in planning and implementing collaborative fishery management plans.

The six collaborative management plans in operation currently encompass six reef closures (subject to periodic reviews) and cover most of the coastline. Some villages have been equipped with radio equipment and patrol boats for enforcement and monitoring. Fishermen have established patrol units in several involved villages to monitor and report incidences of illegal fishing. The navy is also involved in enforcing the protected areas and the program has worked to increase follow-up at the government level for prosecuting dynamite fishermen. Villagers are also involved in data collection and monitoring of reef status and fish counting. The program has implemented gear exchange programs for illegal nets and installed offshore fish aggregating devices to draw fishers away from the reefs. Several attempts have also been made to initiate alternative livelihood programs in participating villages such as mariculture and expansion of seaweed farming. While not all of these initiatives have been successful, the overall structure of adaptive co-management has permitted the communities to learn from mistakes and replicate successes.

Social Endpoint

The poor in Tanzania depend directly on natural resources, such as land, forests, and fisheries, for their livelihoods. The poor are also more vulnerable to degradation of the environmental and natural resource base, which threatens their livelihood and food security. In spite of the relatively high quality of coastal and marine resources that represent potential competitive advantages for Tanzania, a

Photo Paavo Eliste

variety of issues limit the profitability of livelihoods and capture of the full development potential of these assets. These include: (i) inadequate property rights to exploit the resources; (ii) inadequate skills to exploit the resources sustainably; (iii) lack of knowledge about technological improvements and alternative high productivity activities; (iv) inadequate skills and access to the benefits of commercial exploitation of natural resources; (v) inadequate economic incentives for sustainable resource use; and (vi) inadequate infrastructure and markets to make it worthwhile to exploit the resources.

By 2050, it is not unreasonable to expect that poverty will have been completely eliminated in coastal areas. This implies not only improved incomes but also improved access to social and other services. Income sources will be adequately diverse to provide a buffer from sudden shocks, particularly those that might be associated with global or regional environmental change. Local communities will be important players in an adaptive co-management framework that gives them both rights and obligations related to natural resource management and protection.

4 FINANCIAL SUSTAINABILITY

Kumla nguru si kazi,
kazi kumwosha.

It is better to have a permanent
income than to be fascinating.

— Oscar Wilde

Introduction

The importance of "permanent income" has been widely recognized as a key concept in poverty alleviation. Individuals and households with some form of permanent income can better withstand external shocks, they have better health (both mental and physical), and there is less potential for political turmoil engendered by income inequality. It is no accident that – even in market-based economies, even in conservative think-tanks, even among the most ardent right-wing capitalist policy advisors – one finds evidence and sympathy for systems that include some form of minimum permanent income for all individuals or households. Social safety nets through negative taxation, minimum incomes for senior citizens, and unemployment insurance are all acknowledged as efficient and fair devices for achieving human development objectives.

These same lessons can, however, be extrapolated to an institutional scale. Just as the provision of a permanent income to individuals and households achieves some human development objective, permanent income can also be instrumental to the long-term well-being of institutions and the objectives that such institutions seek to achieve. In simple terms, we speak of "financial sustainability" of institutions, but in fact we can extend the corollary between people and institutions to look at four key elements of financial sustainability that we consider in Blueprint 2050.

To many people, the idea of permanent income may simply be that there is a constant flow of money into their pockets, or into their household bank account. Such a view may be a good starting point, but permanent income that addresses some longer term objective (such as human development or achieving an institution's goals) has a more elaborate meaning.

First, the idea of the permanent income must be within the context of *needs*. The needs for an individual may be shelter, food, water, education and health. For an institution involved with marine management, the needs reflect those of maintaining the ecosystem services, paying staff, fueling boats, and building awareness. In economic or financial terms, in either case, we usually seek to meet those needs as cost-effectively as possible. A level of income that is addressing low costs is more likely to be permanent and adequate than if it must address high costs.

Second, permanent income must realistically be realized within the *capacity* of the system. Just as we might not normally expect an unhealthy, frail man to be a productive fisher; we would not expect a degraded, dynamited, fish-less coral reef to attract much interest from tourists. Revenue generation must therefore address two points: improving the capacity of the system to generate revenue, and then capturing the revenue that is generated by that capacity. We heal the man and teach him to fish; that improves his permanent income. We restore the ecosystem and tax the tourists; that improves the system's permanent income.

Third, generating a permanent income for all concerned involves some *sharing among related members*. Within a household, sharing is taken for granted; parents may support children or vice versa, money is mailed to brothers or sisters, all have some security from the capacity of others. Within a managed marine area, sharing of revenues can also ensure that some permanent income is available to all, even if capacity to generate that income may be vested in just a few. Tourism industry, local communities, and local government are all related stakeholders at the ground level; evidence shows that where fair and clear revenue sharing occurs, all benefit immediately and in the longer term. Near-term costs are met, and reinvestment permits improved capacity. A fairly shared pie this year often leads to a larger pie the following year.

Finally, generating a permanent income involves *creating a safety net that relies on broader sharing*. Sometimes external factors affect the income of an entire sub-system. In a household, key income earners may get sick or die. A house may burn down. A crop may fail. To offset this, formal and informal social safety nets can be an important means for ensuring permanent incomes for such misadventures. Friends give assistance. Churches take up donations. Government programs may intervene and give support. Similarly, for marine systems, some areas may be more vulnerable than others and may suffer setbacks that affect all the local stakeholders – a tourism industry, local government, and community members alike. Coral bleaching in some parts of the world affected fishery productivity and tourism revenues. Storms or floods can undermine ecosystem productivity. Political unrest can turn vibrant tourism destinations into ghost towns. But mechanisms are also available for mitigating such effects. Permanent income in a safety net concept involves broadening the sharing over two dimensions: time, and space. Over time, we try to save money to provide a buffer for bad years: a so-called "rainy day" fund. Over space, we pool the risk over un-correlated risk categories. The concept of "un-correlated risk categories" is an important one. It means essentially that we do not put all of our eggs in one basket when thinking of income sources. Drops in tourism receipts from international terrorism fears would likely affect all marine tourist areas, so a simple pooling of tourism receipts may not be adequate to mitigate risks. But in such cases it is likely that people, and international fleets, will keep fishing; thus some pooling of other resource incomes would be a sound strategy. In this chapter, we provide further elaboration on the need and potential for appropriate pooling and risk sharing mechanisms.

Exploring some Concepts – An Economist Speaks

Even in the context of the above four elements of financial sustainability, it is useful to explore in greater depth some of the implications of generating permanent incomes for marine areas. Permanent income in this context is essentially a steady and predictable flow of annual funding sufficient to maintain the quality of the underlying resource base. Experience around the world (some from URT itself) has provided significant insights into what is possible, and what is not possible. But it is not without controversy, and even in the area of financial sustainability much experimentation and learning remains to be done. Let us start with a visit with a local economist and financing expert to look at experience elsewhere.

If you had to define "financial sustainability" in simple terms, where would you start?

It may be easiest to think in terms of profitability. So long as an operation is generating enough income to cover its ongoing costs, it might be regarded as financially sustainable. In the short-term, this means income covers its recurrent operational costs. Over the long-term, income would also need to cover replacement of critical capital equipment. The longer-term view is more relevant to a sustainable operation.

But what if the resource base is slowly deteriorating, even if there are operating profits? Would you regard this as sustainable?

No, it would not be sustainable. But that is why financial sustainability is only one part of capital "S" Sustainability as a whole. A degrading system – whether because the natural resource base is deteriorating or because the social fabric is falling apart – is inherently unsustainable and that in itself will also undermine the longer-term financial sustainability of the system. Some people like to think of Sustainability as a three-legged chair – each leg respectively represents ecological sustainability, financial sustainability, and social sustainability – each leg is necessary. No one or two legs by themselves are sufficient.

It would seem quite difficult then to identify a financially sustainable situation?

It is notoriously difficult. Only many years after the fact might we have some hope of declaring that something was financially sustainable. It is much easier to recognize an "unsustainable" situation than a sustainable one. This gets me back to my point on profitability; if incomes are inadequate to cover recurrent costs, there is definitely a problem and the situation is financially unsustainable. If they are adequate, then the first hurdle towards financial sustainability will have been conquered.

Are there any successful examples of sustainable income generation in protected areas?

There are many in terrestrial systems. The South Africa National Park System has a rather complex structure of tourism-based user fees that finances the entire system. Some high profile parks collect more money than – and subsidize – other parks. Thailand and Costa Rica also use such models. Game park systems in East Africa are working towards similar systems but the costs in some cases are arguably greater than the incomes, especially in the wake of security issues of the sort we have seen lately. In marine areas, the classic case has become Bonaire Marine Park in the Caribbean; the area is entirely self-financing through dive fees that are high enough, in effect, to ration access to the reefs and cause no harmful impacts. Marine parks in South East Asia have also recently significantly increased access fees; often by ten times or more the original values. Although fewer people might come, the drop in numbers is small in comparison to the increased revenues; the positive side-effect is that there is slightly less pressure on the resources. All of these fees are attempting to capture what economists call resource rents.

What are resource rents? Are these the same as profits?

The notion of resource rents stems back to an idea that, to produce something, you need various inputs, or "factors of production." Labor and capital are the classic inputs; tomes of papers, endless negotiations, and countless revolutions have had – at their core – the idea that there is some fair division of the value of production through wages (to labor) and profits (to capital). Purchased intermediate materials, from paperclips to concrete, may also be a necessary input to the production. But natural resources – the land, the clean water, the fish in the sea – can be a key part of the overall value of this production. The value that accrues to these resources is what we can loosely call the "resource rents"; they are like profits, but they are the profits after all of the other inputs have received a fair price. Workers will get a fair wage. Paperclips will have been paid for. Shareholders will have received a normal return on their invested capital. What is left are the resource rents.

Who gets these rents; surely we aren't paying the worms in the dirt or the fish in the sea?

"The rents accrue to the owner of the resource." So the theory says. But one of a few situations might typically arise. First, the resource may have a clear single owner who manages and regulates it well. Not unusually, this owner will be the State. Land is often vested in the State. States lay claim to resources within their EEZ. Second, we might have a clear single owner (such as the State), but that owner does not manage or care for the resource. Finally, there may be no clear ownership, or multiple claims, in which case it is a free-for-all that economists call "open access". Open access is often regarded as the worst of possible situations.

Why should open access be such a bad thing? It seems to me that if a resource is a public good, owned by the State, it should be freely available to anybody and everybody.

You are speaking of the division of the pie, and you are right from that perspective. But the first step in dividing a pie is to make sure that you have, at the start, as big a pie as possible. The problem with free-for-all open access is that it tends to make the pie smaller. The pie in this case is the available resource rent. Over-fishing is the classical example. With open access, as long as there is some profit in it, more people become fishers, they get bigger and expensive boats to outdo each other, they burn up more fuel hunting down fish farther a field. Effort goes up, as do costs, but yield goes down until there is no longer an incentive for more people to become fishers. At that stage, revenues equal costs; there are no exceptional profits or resource rents. We call this rent dissipation. All the potential profits have been eaten up by higher fuel consumption or larger boat investment; and there are fewer fish, so the system ecology has been compromised. There is no longer any pie to divide. If the resource were better managed, through regulated access – for example – the size of the pie would be bigger. The issue then becomes how to share the pie.

On that note, let us take a brief pause before discussing the sharing issue further. I gather that Tanzania already has some experience in generating revenues?

Yes, economists and financial experts undertook an extensive review of current conditions, and – although there are some challenges – the findings are all in all quite promising for the long term.

Financial Sustainability of Marine Reserves in Tanzania

Tanzania has gazetted five Marine Reserves, four of them in the Dar es Salaam area (Bongoyo, Mbudya, Pangavini and Fungu Yasini) and one off the coast of Pangani district (Maziwi). In total, the Reserves protect just under 30 km². All marine reserves in Tanzania are no-take zones for fishing and other extractive activities; tourism activities are permitted.

Private operators have been ferrying tourists to and from the islands since the late 1980s. The private operators have assisted local people to establish food and beverage services on Mbudya and Bongoyo; Pangavini remains relatively untouched by human influence because of its rocky shoreline.

The Marine Parks and Reserves Unit (MPRU) has agreed to allow the local people to continue their vending services on the islands, has provided them with training, and has made them honorary wardens.

Bongoyo and Mbudya receive significant visitor arrivals, particularly on weekends, because of their white, clean sandy beaches and close proximity to the urban and tourist areas of Dar es Salaam. The MPRU has erected signboards, built basic latrines and cut trails on Bongoyo to facilitate day tourism. Visitors pay US$10 for the day ($5 for transport, $5 for Reserve entry fee). The MPRU operates one boat a few times per month to patrol the Dar Reserves, and a MPRU staff member is present on the islands every day to ensure compliance with entry fee requirements.

The Reserves are most likely generating enough revenue to sustain themselves, particularly given the active participation of the honorary wardens. Entry and user fees are adequate to finance weekly patrols as well as staff on the islands. Over time, small investments could be made in tourism infrastructure to enhance visitor experience and enable higher fees to be charged.

The Reserves are most likely financially sustainable given existing entry fees and visitation levels. However, if part of a system, private sector concessions for one or two of the islands could significantly meet the financing requirements of other components of that system.

Point of Departure

Background

Internationally, many MPAs face financial constraints as government funding is reduced from already low levels, and costs increase as natural areas are subjected to greater pressures. An additional challenge for MPAs in developing countries is that MPAs are often supported through donor programs for start up and investments. This donor support is a double-edged sword: it overcomes often seemingly formidable start-up hurdles, but it also can engender a donor dependency that makes it difficult to commit seriously to diversifying income sources and reducing costs; capital purchased in the early years will still need maintenance and replacement once the initial funding is exhausted. The MPAs in Tanzania and Zanzibar face similar challenges.

Most of the protected areas are still relatively young, and the management approaches and sustainable financing strategies are all in the making. Further, the MPAs and MMAs in mainland Tanzania and Zanzibar islands provide a broad range of early experiences and lessons on which to build a future system. The discussion that follows summarizes some of the revenue, cost, and sharing issues that are important to financial sustainability.

Typical Revenues and Sources of Funding

Protected areas in developing countries typically tap three primary sources of funding: government, international donors, and self-generating activities. Tanzania is no exception. Government determines the need for the establishment of a protected area and often turns to development partners (e.g., multilateral development institutions, bilateral aid agencies, or international conservation NGOs) for both technical and financial assistance. The funding arrangements (and often how those resources can be used) for each site are determined largely by the requirements of the donors. Our surveys show that donors often provide some 80 to 90 percent of total funds available for the establishment and operation of the protected area. Government and revenue-generating activities at the site itself contribute the remaining 10 to 20 percent (Figure 4.1). Government typically finances salaries of government staff and basic recurrent costs (e.g.,

consumables, utilities, etc.). Revenue generating activities can include entry and user fees, or licensing and taxation (Table 4.1). Many projects typically include the development of self-generating revenue schemes as part of the overall project approach, primarily to ensure the sustainability of activities that the project is initiating.

It is interesting that most donor-funded projects tend to be of similar size, scope and duration, at the design stage. A typical project will focus on one geographic area of 800 km^2, and cost up to US$500 000 per year for 5 years. Most projects tend to be extended, though some donors are more amenable to extensions than others.

Figure 4.1   Source of funds of protected areas in Zanzibar

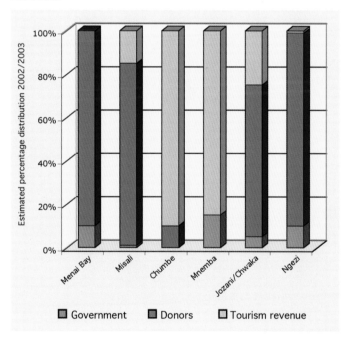

Table 4.1   Tanzania Marine Park (MP) and Marine Reserve (MR) fee structure, 2003

Entrance fee per person per day	Citizen	Non-citizen
>16 years of age	TSh1 000	US$10 (MP) US$ 5 (MR)
5 to 16 years of age	TSh200	US$ 5 (MP) US$ 3 (MR)
<5 years of age	Free	Free
Boat and Sport Fishing Licenses (MP)		
Boats powered by ≤40 hp engine trading in marine resources	Tsh10 000 per month	
Boats powered >40hp engine trading in marine resources	Tsh50 000 per month	
Visiting Leisure Boats privately owned and non-commercial	US$10 per entry for maximum 7 d	
Visiting Commercial Leisure Boats, including charters	US$50 per entry for maximum 7 d	
Game Fishing Boat	US$50 per entry up to 7 d	
Cruise Ship/Tourist Passenger Boat	US$500 per entry	
Visitors staying in lodges and either fishing in a boat owned by a registered business in the marine parks, or fishing in a visiting game fishing boat, shall pay a fishing license.	US$20 for period of 7 d	
Fishermen on Game Fishing Boat	US$50 per person up to 7 d	
Boat and Sport Fishing Licenses (MR)		
Passenger boats with carrying capacity of 15 passengers	US$200 per month	
Local registered Leisure Boat	TSh5 000 per month	
Foreign registered Leisure Boat	US$40 per month	
Concession (MR Only)		
Concession to operate public services (e.g., restaurants)	US$2 400 per year or US$200 per month	
Commercial Filming Fees (MP & MR)		
Image capture of any type (still photography, motion picture photography, conventional video imaging)	US$500 for up to 14 d	

Cost Structures

Costs for park operation differ depending on site characteristics and local management objectives. The variation is evident in Zanzibar (Table 4.2) where both the direct costs and the average costs (per unit of area) can span a range of two orders of magnitude. There is also variation in how the funds are distributed across cost categories (Table 4.3). A frequent remark, confirmed by these findings, is that the proportion dedicated to field operations is too low (at times no greater than 5 percent) while operational expenses on staff and foreign technical assistance consultants is too high (as high as 45 percent) to be financially sustainable over the long term.

Table 4.2   Estimated annual operational costs for protected areas in Zanzibar, 2003

Site	Size (km²)	Operating Budget US$	Costs/km² US$
Menai Bay	470	85 000	181
Misali	22	120 000	5 454
Chumbe	1	21 600	21 600
Mnemba	12	5 000	417
Jozani/ Chwaka	50	430 000	8 600
Ngezi	14.4	30 000	2 083
Kiwengwa	17.5	13 356	763

Photo Dean Housden

Table 4.3   Estimated allocations of project expenditures in protected areas in Tanzania mainland, 2003

Expenditure Category	Description	Range of Total Cost
Personnel & Consultants	Salaries and benefits for international technical advisors and national staff; fees for specific technical consultancies.	30 – 45 %
Community Development	Alternative income generating activities (beekeeping, mariculture, fish ponds) or revolving loan schemes (fishing gear, business loans).	0 –15 %
Workshops, Training & Travel	Capacity building activities for staff and target population; workshops for training, awareness or project monitoring and evaluation; travel for national, regional or international workshops and training; staff home leave.	10 –15 %
Office Running Costs	Rent, utilities, communications, consumables, management fees of implementing agencies.	10 – 15 %
Field Running Costs	Field activities such as reef monitoring, installation of moorings and buoys, enforcement patrols, fish counts, licensing activities, fuel and maintenance costs.	5 – 30 %
Capital costs	Infrastructure (office or boat-house buildings, staff housing, slipways) and equipment (4WD vehicles, boats, engines, computers, SCUBA gear).	15 – 30 %

Photo Paavo Eliste

Let us pick up now where we left off with our local economist and go back to this sharing idea. You mentioned earlier that in other places, there was some pooling of funds to finance entire systems.

That's right. Some call this cross-subsidization, some call it pooling. Financial mechanisms – like taxes, user fees, or voluntary donations – go into a common pool that is used to finance all functions across all parts of the system. The pool of funds can either be part of the normal operational budgets of an institution or, where circumstances warrant, it may make sense to operate through a specially designed trust fund. Such trust funds are becoming more common. Uganda has one to look after its Gorilla parks. Namibia has a national fund to redistribute income from game licensing and one-off sales of ivory.

Selling elephant ivory to finance protected areas! Is that not controversial?

In that particular instance, the sales were carefully monitored by CITES and were part of an international experiment in controlled ivory trade. There was a significant windfall for countries that participated in this experiment. But, of greater relevance, is the idea that you might sacrifice some small part of your assets to pay for the protection of an entire system. Protected area managers – in terrestrial and marine systems – are often confronted with this quandary. If culling some elephants to generate ivory sales can finance the core expenses of the system, and if such culling is ecologically sustainable and socially necessary to limit human-animal conflicts, some argue that it makes sense to do that. Similarly, entire areas can be "sacrificed" to high value tourism or commercial development, if such values generate income that can be effectively channeled to protect other areas.

In Tanzania, I have heard that there are proposals to develop some of the offshore islands by giving them over to private investors. Is this what you mean by sacrificing areas?

Yes and no. (Being an economist permits me to say both yes and no at the same time.) Yes: because turning such places over to private investment might preclude other conservation uses. No: because individual sites are not necessarily worse off after such a turnover. Much depends on the circumstances of the deal, and the type of management plan contemplated for the area. Typically, arrangements are such that investors are compelled to follow a management plan and if they fail to do so, they lose their lease rights at time of renewal or – in extreme cases – immediately.

The idea of sacrificial areas seems somewhat abstract. Can you give any practical examples.

Two come to mind: Sentosa Island off Singapore, and Hanauma Bay in Hawaii. Both are well known tourist sites. Sentosa is accessible from downtown Singapore within 30 minutes by any casual visitor, offering beaches, an amusement park, a train, walking paths, grassy areas and gardens, and a marine exhibit offering turtles, a huge pelagic tank, and an undersea tunnel experience on a moving carpet. Sentosa attracts millions of visitors annually, and there are only remnants left of the original ecosystem. But financial proceeds from the island contribute to research, monitoring and enforcement of the rest of Singapore's offshore islands that now still have pristine beaches, intact coral, and a local fishery, even though these islands are in one of the busiest shipping lanes in the world. Sentosa might be sacrificed, but many argue that even Sentosa's degraded ecological conditions are better than adjacent sites in Singapore Harbor.

Hanauma Bay is another classic example. It is a naturally protected shallow bay about 30 minutes by bus from Hawaii's busy Waikiki Beach tourism development, and less than an hour from Honolulu's commercial center. Millions of people have had their first snorkeling experience in Hanauma Bay, feeding fish, inhaling saltwater, standing on the reef flats. Twenty years ago the site was approaching an ecological disaster, with municipal and state authorities haggling over an ever-diminishing pie. Common sense prevailed at a certain point, and the area was temporarily closed while a sustainable management plan was thought through and implemented. These days, Hanauma Bay boasts conservation education exhibits, limits vehicle access, provides lessons in "sustainable snorkeling", and still attracts hundreds of thousands of visitors annually who pay premium prices for access to the site. Ongoing research activities monitor reef health and recovery in this "multiple use" area. Ecological conditions have recovered considerably, albeit not to the pristine conditions that my colleague the ecologist might want to see. But the park generates significant amounts of cash. That cash now finances almost the entire Oahu Island park system, and even contributes to local bus subsidies. Many of Oahu's parks would not otherwise have been able to afford the type of conservation efforts they now enjoy. The system as a whole is in better shape.

Is it not risky to rely on a single site like this?

Yes, these may be regarded as extreme examples to show my point. Ideally you would want enough diversity of income to shelter you from problems at a single site. Diversity means more than just having different sources of income; it also means that such sources are subject to uncorrelated risks. If all of your income sources are just different ways of taxing tourists, then it does little good if the tourism market is all of a sudden shocked. Some parks in Indonesia generate revenue from geothermal power stations within their boundaries; these are hooked into a few particularly hot energy sources and generate power – and royalties – even if tourists stop coming for a while. This sort of robustness is what we are looking for in a financially sustainable system.

So from this discussion, I take away that financial sustainability includes aspects of profitability, paying attention to long-term conditions, sharing revenues and risks, and potentially making some sacrifices for a greater good. How do Tanzania's prospects measure up on these accounts?

Your summary is correct. The most important lesson we have from experience elsewhere is that we need to keep financial sustainability of the system as a whole in our sights. To alter slightly a common saying: "Think systemically, act locally." As for Tanzania's prospects, the biggest historical failing is that not enough attention has been paid to such systemic thinking. Although Tanzania has an impressive portfolio of experience with different methods at different sites, few attempts have been made to pull this together into local networks or larger sub-systems. Individual sites are then more vulnerable than they need to be, and considerable opportunities are lost. But this also suggests that there is an excellent starting point for developing a financially sustainable system.

Sharing and Pooling Mechanisms

The ability to share or pool resources depends both on the capture of potential revenue sources, and on the availability of institutional arrangements to distribute revenues. In principle, in both the Tanzania mainland and Zanzibar, formal pooling mechanisms exist that would permit redistribution of revenues.

On the mainland, a Conservation and Development Fund established under the Marine Parks and Reserves Act is such an instrument. More formally called the "Marine Parks and Reserves Revolving Fund", it serves as a repository for:

- All funding received from the Government for use within or relating to the Marine Parks and Reserves Unit (MPRU) or any marine park or reserve.

- All voluntary subscriptions, donations or bequests received by the MPRU or any marine park or reserve from any source.

- All proceeds from user and entry fees, tourism levies, proceeds from licensing fees and other charges imposed by the Marine Parks and Reserves Act in respect of the use, and development, of any activities in a marine park or reserve.

- Revenue from the sustainable resource use or development activities conducted by the MPRU.

- Any other sum or property which may be vested in the MPRU or a marine park or reserve as a result of the performance of its functions.

On Zanzibar, a similar fund is established under the Environmental Management for Sustainable Development Act. The National Fund for Protected Areas may be used for purposes of protecting, enhancing and managing the national protected areas system in Zanzibar.

Memorandums of understanding or similar arrangements can also be used to share or pool incomes. Two examples from the mainland demonstrate both the potential benefits and the implementation challenges of developing such arrangements.

The *Tanga Program* investigated the issue of poor revenue collection from fisheries by local government. It estimated that no more than 25 percent of potential revenues are currently being collected, with some estimates as low as 5 percent. Tanga municipality collected US$15 000 in calendar year 2002 (representing about 40 percent of expected revenue for the year). It could potentially collect from US$60 000 to US$300 000 each year. As each MMA costs roughly US$30 000 to operate per year, the municipality could sustainably manage both its MMAs solely from revenue collected from the fisheries sector.

To identify methods of improving revenue collection, the Tanga Program is currently designing a pilot initiative that will test a permit system. Tests will most likely be in Pangani district due to its manageable size. The Fisheries Act gives the legal authority to local government to collect revenues from fisheries products (central government collects export duties and fees from vessels over 11 m in length). How local governments collect these revenues is up to them, so there is scope to test different modalities of collection.

At the *Mafia Island Marine Park (MIMP)*, the role of the Mafia District Council (MDC) deserves attention. To date, there is no formal agreement between the park and MDC that establishes co-management structures or revenue-sharing mechanisms, among other things. The Act does not make specific statements about the role of local government, except to say that they should receive a share of net revenues and be represented in decision-making. The overall financing pool available is, in principle, quite substantial, but the MDC feels that it gets inadequate financial support compared to the MIMP. The district generated about US$70 000 of its own revenues, plus received about US$761 000 in external subventions; MIMP by contrast generated about US$60 000 of its own revenues, plus received about US$450 000 in external subventions in 2003.

Within this context, there is at present little in the way of coordinated planning between local district and park authorities. For example, on one occasion, the park's Board of Trustees reviewed the MDC Development Plan, selected one item for one of the MIMP villages – a dispensary in Juani village – and proceeded to fund that activity (it is unclear to the MDC whether this was meant to be part of revenue-sharing agreement with the MDC or the village, or why this particular village was selected). MDC feels that even though the activity was included in the District Development Plan, the MDC itself should have been able to determine how MIMP funds would be used. According to the MDC, the dispensary was not the biggest priority for the district at that time.

In addition to planning issues, the actual sharing of benefits remains a controversial issue. MDC does not collect any fees or taxes from the hotels located inside the MIMP. Hotels pay 20 percent VAT directly to Treasury; these hotels account for the largest percentage of VAT collected in Mafia, followed by small shops. Hotels do not pay any concessions for operating inside the Park, primarily because many of the hotels were there before the park was established.

Some Case Studies

Mnazi Bay – Ruvuma Estuary Marine Park

Starting in 1998, a series of discussions in Mtwara district led to the "Mtwara Declaration," in which the district authorities at both governmental and civil society levels agreed to the creation of a marine park in the Mnazi Bay area. This agreement came from 17 villages (consisting of about 30 000 people), through ward and division levels to the district. At the district level it was approved by both the district council and by the relevant authorities of government. Agreement was reached on an outer boundary, which was then approved by the region, followed by the central government where the Ministry put it to Parliament under the Marine Parks and Reserves framework legislation. The Mnazi Bay – Ruvuma Estuary Marine Park (MB-REMP) was officially gazetted in 2000.

Communities in Mtwara district are very poor, relying primarily on subsistence fishing and agriculture for their survival. Per capita incomes are less than US$100 per year. Facilities to support organized tourism do not exist. Although Mtwara has an airport with regular flights to Dar es Salaam, tourism is not yet a factor in the district economy. But there are signs that this may change with the recent

development of a small luxury hotel in Mikindani. Besides tourism, the national government has plans to develop southern Tanzania by improving transport links and other infrastructure. This is the proposed Mtwara Development Corridor, a collaborative effort involving the governments of Malawi, Mozambique and Tanzania. The corridor is designed to promote investment in infrastructure including transportation, industry and tourism. Transboundary initiatives are to be prioritized. Because a reliable power supply is vital for the area, development includes a proposal to upgrade the power generation plant at Mtwara. One option under consideration is a gas-to-electricity project utilizing natural gas resources in the vicinity of Mnazi Bay.

A US$3 million GEF financed and UNDP implemented project is developing a multi-purpose MPA around the globally significant marine biodiversity values of the Mnazi Bay and Ruvuma River estuary areas in southern Tanzania. The 54 month project emphasizes the sustainable use of marine resources by communities, as well as biodiversity conservation. It includes an initial participatory planning phase (30 months) followed by a 2 year implementation phase. During the first two years of the project, roughly 93 percent of the US$530 000 required annually is provided by external donors.

The project places a strong emphasis on building partnerships among its stakeholders, achieving financial self-sufficiency, and providing long-term socioeconomic benefits to the local communities that depend on the resources of the site. In so doing, it seeks to establish a self-reliant MPA management capacity. The MP-REMP Board will appoint and fund all MPRU staff while district authorities will support the MPA through in-kind staff commitments. The project will help the Board to generate additional revenue to meet ongoing operating costs through a Sustainable Financing Strategy. All revenues will be used solely for purposes related to park management. The costs of management inputs and external funding will be minimized by building local stakeholder support and utilizing local voluntary contributions to supplement work by paid staff. The MPRU and local stakeholders will undertake collaborative management and monitoring programs.

Based on current information, the costs and revenues for the MB-REMP can be projected through 2012 (Figure 4.2). In year three of the project (end-2004), the Board on behalf of government has committed to provide roughly US$75 000 funding annually for all marine park staff (except the international technical advisor). In comparison, the current annual funding for Mafia marine park staff is US$35 000.

Figure 4.2   Cost and revenue projections for Mnazi Bay – Ruvuma Estuary Marine Park, 2003–2012

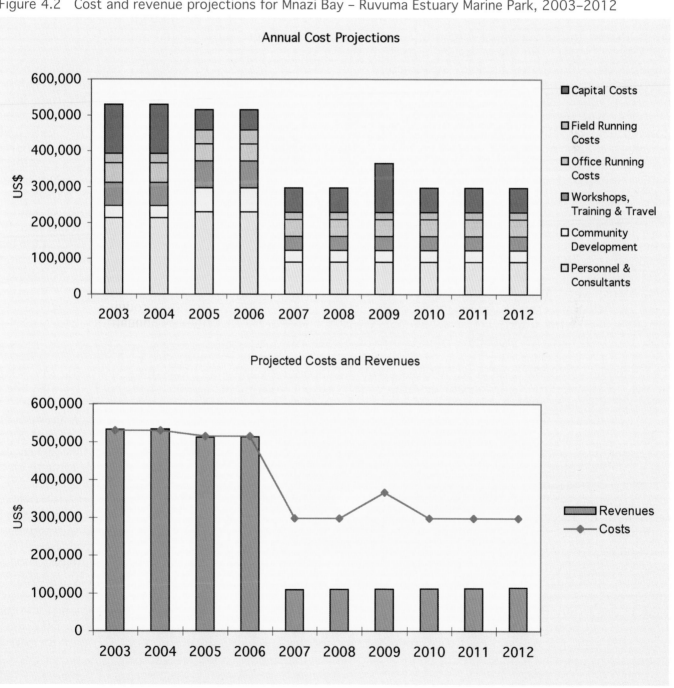

The government has also committed to meet the ongoing costs of managing the park at the conclusion of the project. This commitment could cost roughly US$140 000 annually beginning in 2007, and almost US$200 000 in 2010 for capital replacement or major maintenance. These are conservative estimates and may be much higher in reality.

In the short-term, the park has sufficient funding from donors and government commitments to pay for selected staff. But some issues regarding the medium and long-term financial sustainability of the park deserve further attention. It will experience severe revenue shortages when donor funding is reduced at the end of 2006, based on current commitments. Unlike some other MPAs, tourism revenues cannot be expected to cover substantial percentages of operating costs; tourism is minimal and is hampered by poor infrastructure, lack of marketing, and cheaper alternative locations. The potential for granting concessions for oil or gas exploration may exist but is not guarantied at this point in time. Further, the local revenue collection system for fishing licenses and taxes on marine products has not been extensively developed. In sum, there is very little revenue the park can generate itself in the short-term. In the longer term, the best prospect lies with improving revenue collection from the local fisheries industry.

The extent to which the local government is involved in benefit distribution will largely determine how effective the park will be in generating revenue locally. While the MPRU has the legal mandate to collect entry and user fees within the park, local government is legally mandated to issue fishing licenses and collect taxes on marine products. Given (i) current low levels of tourist arrivals and slow growth projections for the medium- and long-term; and (ii) the uncertainty of concessions for oil exploitation, local government is in the best position to generate, and retain, revenue. A promising option might be the establishment of a comprehensive and workable licensing and taxation system for marine and coastal activities, in conjunction with a district MMA Fund to retain a portion of those revenues. The licensing and taxation system would not be limited to the park area, nor would the activities financed out of the MMA Fund be limited to park boundaries.

Over the longer term, MB-REMP staff, in close collaboration with central and local government and the private sector, should proactively pursue opportunities in developing tourism products, services and infrastructure, along with oil or gas exploration and exploitation. If a dependable revenue base that is sufficient to cover core operating costs is established from the licensing and taxation system, increased tourism or mineral revenues can help finance larger, more capital intensive, investments.

Without increased revenues from tourism or mineral exploitation, alternative external financing will be needed for capital investments over the long-term for government to meet its financial commitments. This might also be achieved by a pooled fund that takes advantage of revenues generated nationally from other marine park areas or from other revenue sources (such as deep sea fisheries or offshore oil and gas concessions). A key to the park's long-term financial sustainability is the inclusion and meaningful participation of local government in cost and benefit sharing. This will require a substantial transfer of autonomy and power to local government and communities and continued support, both technically and financially, from central government.

Menai Bay Conservation Area

Menai Bay in the southwest of Unguja is a traditional fishing ground with extensive coral reefs, sea grass beds, mangrove forests, and coral islands. The coastal and marine resources remained relatively undisturbed until the early 1990s when the use of destructive fishing methods became prominent. The increasing demand for food in the cities of Dar es Salaam and Zanzibar is a major driving force behind the depletion of the fishing grounds.

Following an increase of fishermen – both resident and visiting – in the bay, the traditional management of the area, which enabled resources to be harvested on a sustainable basis, virtually collapsed. The traditional system included temporary (seasonal) closure of fishing areas, and the control of fishing gear and visiting fishermen. The consequences of the collapse in this system were realized by the fishermen of the Fumba peninsula in 1992 and they formed a management committee comprising representatives from four villages. Over a period of three years the

Tourism in a Community Conservation Area.

About 12 000 tourists visited the Menai Bay Conservation Area in 2002. There is already some tourism infrastructure in the area. There are restaurants and lodges such as Beach Villa, Dolphin View, and Sea Villa at Kizimkazi-Mkunguni; and Cabs and Kizidi Restaurants at Kizimkazi-Dimbani in the south. Nyemembe Sea Safari operates in the central districts, while Fumba Sea Safari and Adventures Afloat operate in the west. Most of the activities such as dolphin viewing, boat tours, camping on the islands, and provision of lunches to visitors are conducted by these operators in collaboration with international and local tour operators. Local tour operators charge around

Departments of Fisheries and Environment worked together closely with the management committee, identifying problems and ways to resolve them. The management committee gained no formal or legal recognition but represented a valuable first step towards empowering communities to manage their own resources. For the first six months of implementation, the four villages raised their own funds to provide fuel for the patrols and volunteered personnel to different activities.

At this stage the Department of Fisheries approached WWF for possible assistance to take the process forward. A workshop in 1995 brought together all stakeholders to discuss resource management issues in the bay. A decline of marine resources was seen by the communities to be a major threat to their livelihood. The communities felt positive towards the initial management system in the Fumba area where they were involved in decision-making, and they wanted to extend the system to include the larger Menai Bay area. WWF decided to support a three year project, initially focusing on baseline studies of the area's ecological and socio-economic status, as well as boundary surveys. Preparatory work included education and awareness programs, and the establishment of a management unit to patrol and engage in different activities.

Menai Bay Conservation Area (MBCA) was declared in 1997 under the Fisheries Act of 1988, covering 470 km^2 – the largest MPA in Zanzibar. The objective of MBCA is sustainable use – regulated fishing with non-destructive gears, tourism activities and sustainable mangrove harvesting – for the benefit of local communities.

The management system of MBCA operates at the village, district and national levels. MBCA has three administrative districts and two regions, with a population of about 27 000. To involve the 21 local communities, village conservation committees have been established in all villages. In each village there are ten democratically elected committee members responsible for all environmental affairs in the area. The committee works in close collaboration with the Shehas and a fisheries officer based in the village. The committees are comprised of both men and women of different ages irrespective of education and social status. Because of the large number of villages it is a challenging task to build a community-based institution capable of coherently supporting and managing conservation activities.

A unit consisting of around 15 staff seconded from the Department of Fisheries has the day-to-day management responsibility of the area. The unit is located in the Department of Fisheries in Zanzibar Town. Two patrol officers work from a temporary field office on the southern border of the bay; they patrol the area, record fish catch data, engage in environmental education activities, and train local fishermen in patrolling techniques. Since the area is so large, the plan is eventually to have three field stations from which officers will patrol and engage communities.

From initial investments, the area has most of the capital equipment needed for maintaining the basic level of operation. The total operating budget for MBCA for 2003 was about US$75 000, 90 percent is from WWF; the balance is from the Government of Zanzibar. Revenue collection in previous years would have covered approximately half of the operating costs. Projections suggest that MBCA could approach financial sustainability, covering operating costs by 2007. This would not, however, be adequate for full capital replacement of boats, engines, and other equipment and infrastructure.

The management of MBCA has started work on strategies for the sustainable financing of its operations. A tourism revenue collection scheme was drawn up in 2001 for MBCA, and implementation commenced in 2004. In addition, a bylaw from 2001 sets out a fee structure and entrenches the principle of 100 percent revenue retention for MBCA: 70 percent of the revenue collected from the area is to be used for management, 30 percent is to be used for development of community activities proposed by the District Committee. But significant challenges remain. Menai Bay is not one of the priority areas of the Zanzibar Tourism Master Plan, which are the northern and the south eastern zones of Unguja, and the northern and western zones in Pemba. This may hamper tourism growth potential in the area because infrastructure development may be delayed.

Chumbe Island

Chumbe Island Coral Park Ltd. (CHICOP) was established in 1991 as a privately funded and managed reef and forest conservation project covering the whole of Chumbe Island (0.2 km^2) and the 1 km fringing reef on its western side. Chumbe is located approximately 12 km south west of Zanzibar Town, 6 km from the nearest point on Unguja. The coral reef is acknowledged as one of the most pristine in the region, with 370 species of fish and over 200 species of reef-building corals. In addition, the coral communities in the sanctuary survived the bleaching event in 1998 relatively unscathed. The forest covering the island is one of the last pristine coral rag forests in Zanzibar and has now become a sanctuary for the endangered Aders' duiker, trans-located from Unguja where it is facing extinction from poaching and habitat destruction. The island has a large population of the potentially endangered coconut crab, and a large breeding population of rare roseate terns.

The reef on the western side of the island was protected as a marine sanctuary in 1994 and the forest, as a "closed forest." CHICOP entered into management agreements with the Government of Zanzibar for the management of both the island and the reef.

The management agreement for the reef sanctuary establishes an advisory committee with representatives from the government and villages, as well as other resource people, to advise CHICOP on the management of the area. The day-to-day management of the island and the reefs is the responsibility of CHICOP. Rangers paid by CHICOP are stationed on the island, and they regularly patrol the single no-take zone. Impacts have been positive: incursions have gone down from as many as 45 incidents per month in 1994 to under 10 throughout all of 2002. Personnel stationed on the island tend to the needs of tourists and visiting researchers. The main activities for tourists are guided snorkel trips, forest walks, and beach recreation.

CHICOP operated an extensive environmental education program over the last few years. The first phase started in 1999 and involved the participation of teachers from three schools, staff from the Department of Fisheries, the Institute of Marine Science (IMS), the SOS school, and the staff of Chumbe Island. In 2000, a total of 226 secondary students were taken to the island. Phase 2 of the school excursions started in 2001, and there are plans that by 2003 all 35 secondary schools in Zanzibar will have participated in the program. CHICOP commissioned a qualified teacher trainer as the school coordinator, to help develop the excursions into a more systematic practical one-day course on coral reef ecology and conservation for Form I and II of Secondary Education.

Since CHICOP started its tourist operation in 1998, most of the operational costs have been financed through tourism revenues. It generally sells two types of packages: (a) overnight stays with all activities, accommodation and board included with prices from US$100 to US$200; and, (b) day trips including snorkel trips, forest walks, and lunch, with prices from US$50 to US$70.

At the initiation of operations, financial studies showed that a net, all-inclusive overnight price (excluding agents' commissions) of US$200 per person and an occupancy rate of at least 41 percent was needed to reach the break-even-point for running costs without capital payback. While in good years such targets might be achievable, an MPA that is wholly reliant on tourism receipts is vulnerable to external factors such as security concerns.

Unlike community co-management initiatives, CHICOP is a private tourist operator and is subject to corporate taxation. The number and level of taxes are important to consider in a strategy that aims to involve the private sector in management of MPAs. CHICOP pays a number of taxes and fees, or collects and remits these on behalf of others:

- Hotel levy on all revenue is 15 percent of total receipts. Sales tax on all sales revenue (restaurant, transfers, etc.) is an additional 10 percent of the total. Stamp duty is 1.5 percent.

- Zanzibar Social Security fund contribution is normally regarded as part of salary overheads. This compulsory pension plan takes 5 percent of all employees' pay while CHICOP, as a company, must add 10 percent of the wage bill as its contribution.

- Income tax on staff salary depends on the pay scale and is deducted from the pay at source.

- Fees include an annual land lease of US$4 900, a hotel license of US$400, a boutique license of US$200, and permits for international workers of US$120 each.

- Purchases of supplies and goods are charged a 20 percent VAT.

- Corporate tax is zero for not-for-profit operators and between 30 percent and 50 percent for companies. Payments have been in dispute because of the taxation status of CHICOP.

CHICOP is an innovative project gaining acclaim internationally among tourism and conservation circles for its achievements. The reef is in excellent condition, serving as an aquarium and laboratory for visitors and researchers of all kinds. The tourism numbers and impacts are low and well within the carrying capacity of the fragile island environment. Further, the coral rag forest is becoming an important habitat for Zanzibar's endemic Ader's duiker. Financial sustainability is hampered, however, by the lack of clarity in financial terms, and the lack of diversity in revenue sources.

Synopsis – Towards a Marine Legacy Fund

Financial sustainability needs attention. While Tanzania and Zanzibar have significant experience in different MPA and MMA models, the financial sustainability of these models is far from secure. To date, the general trend is that sites operate in isolation, with little or no regard for linking them as a network or a system. Individual sites are characterized by extreme dependency on external financing that is not guaranteed in perpetuity (Figure 4.3), and at times imposes high cost structures that will themselves be difficult to finance.

As a first reaction, one might legitimately ask whether this external dependency is out of the ordinary. To place it in perspective, it is instructive to consider Tanzania's national budget. Recent trends have seen steady decreases in external dependency. In 2002/03, the entire national government budget was financed 47 percent by foreign assistance. In 2003/04 this had declined to 45 percent and the 2004/05 budget figures project 41 percent. From this perspective, the 87 percent dependency of marine parks on foreign assistance seems disproportionately high.

But addressing financial sustainability needs to take a multi-pronged approach:

Cost reduction is an obvious first step. This is achievable through different means. Surveys show that personnel, especially foreign technical assistance, remains one of the highest direct costs in marine management in Tanzania. Long term financial sustainability will require that these high cost resources be replaced by more cost-effective local expertise. Fortunately, Tanzania's pool of skilled labor is growing, but more training will no doubt be necessary to achieve Blueprint 2050 targets.

Another means of changing cost structures is to rely more on *co-management models* that permit private sector or community participation. Evidence shows that including private sector partners and communities within the overall management framework will reduce overall costs, while also achieving ecological and social equity goals. Distributional issues – whether they relate to taxation or benefit sharing – remain one of the more difficult issues in achieving financial sustainability.

More *diversified revenue generation* is the next step in achieving financial sustainability. At present, tourism revenue remains the principle target for covering operational costs. But relying on such a single source of revenue is little different than relying on foreign donor assistance. It is more appropriate to rely on a diversity of sectors and mechanisms.

It is time to think systemically. Areas such as Mnazi Bay may never be financially sustainable by themselves, but they warrant being included as an important part of a national system. Financing must also therefore look at more extensive pooling of resources, from a diversity of sources. Many analysts propose local revenue pooling schemes, which are accessible by districts, local communities, and MPA or MMA authorities themselves. Such local pools can themselves in turn be connected to higher level funds. Indeed, we have seen that national legislation both in Zanzibar and Tanzania mainland provides for the establishment of higher level pooling mechanisms.

Using a high level fund – let us call it a Marine Legacy Fund – has been discussed informally in Tanzania on numerous occasions. While implementation of such an idea within short-term planning horizons seems onerous, it is a perfectly reasonable goal as part of a fifty year vision. Is a Marine Legacy Fund practical? How large should it be, and what are the potential revenue sources? To answer these questions, we must recognize that the goal of the fund is to act as a conduit for collecting and redistributing revenues, and for acting as a buffer during bad years. This is quite different from an "endowment arrangement" in which a fixed amount of capital generates interest payments which finance the core costs of the system. We estimate that the core costs of a system in Tanzania and Zanzibar would be of the order of US$6 million annually, covering approximately 30 core MPAs or MMAs. An endowment fund with no revenue sources generating a 5 percent return on capital invested would need to be US$120 million in size to cover those costs. But the Marine Legacy Fund would not operate this way: it would collect and redistribute revenues on an annual basis, relying on a diversity of revenue sources (including some operating interest on fund capital). It would need to be able to weather a few years of income shortfalls, and the value of the Fund could thus fluctuate over a broader range of values. But because it is not an endowment, its target value could be somewhat less than that of an endowment fund.

Menu of Financing Options.

Numerous mechanisms are available for generating or collecting revenue within a single MPA or MMA, or within a system of networks of MPAs and MMAs.

Tourism: entrance fees, hotel taxes, shares of VAT, joint venture shares, concession fees.

Commercial, Sports or Artisanal fisheries: license fees, fines, area leases, boat fees, trophy fees, export royalties, concession fees (sports).

Oil, Gas or Mineral Concessions: development permits, concession fees, production royalties, compensation payments through offsets.

Research: permit fees, photography fees, exports, joint venture agreements on bioprospecting.

Coastal land or island development: lease or outright sale, profit shares.

Other global support: direct conservation payments, offsets, donations.

Figure 4.3   Financial sustainability indicators for three Tanzania mainland sites

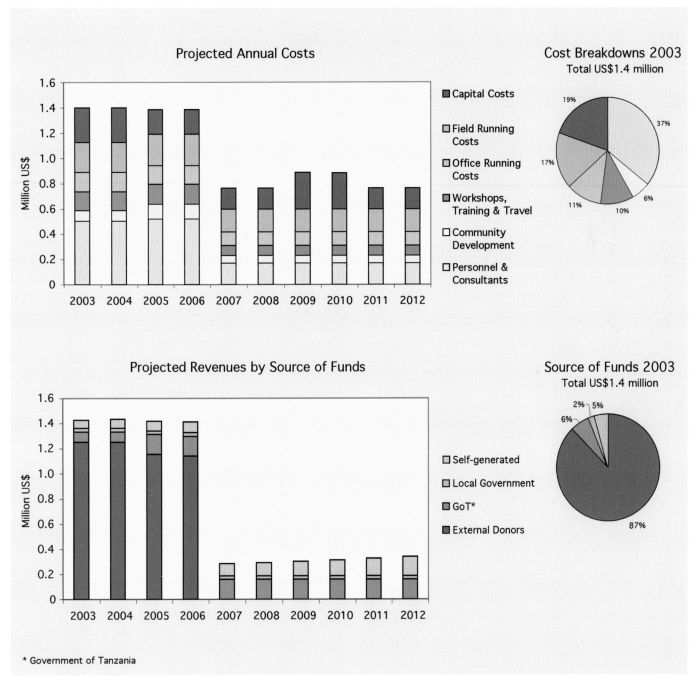

Projected Annual Costs

- Capital Costs
- Field Running Costs
- Office Running Costs
- Workshops, Training & Travel
- Community Development
- Personnel & Consultants

Cost Breakdowns 2003
Total US$1.4 million

Projected Revenues by Source of Funds

- Self-generated
- Local Government
- GoT*
- External Donors

Source of Funds 2003
Total US$1.4 million

* Government of Tanzania

A survey of three sites (Mafia Island Marine Park, Mnazi Bay – Ruvuma Estuary Marine Park, Tanga Coastal Zone Conservation and Development Program) on the Tanzania mainland shows a general pattern of potential financial non-sustainability. Some 87 percent of the US$1.4 million financing to these three sites is being provided by external donors. As all current donor-funded projects are scheduled to close at the end of 2006, the medium- to long-term picture suggests that financing sources will only cover about one half of the typical on-going operational costs.

We estimate that an adequate fund level would be approximately US$50 million, with operating fluctuations from US$25 million to US$100 million. This would be adequate to cover an annual US$6 million operational cost outflow, with annual average inflows to the fund of US$3 million (the balance of US$3 million is internally generated). This scale would also permit a 4 year hiatus in inflows. The operational question then becomes: Is it possible to expect US$3 million of inflow into the Marine Legacy Fund? To put this in perspective, let us translate this into some physical measures from three lead sectors that might conceivably contribute to such inflows.

- Tourism. MPA entrance fees are up to US$10 a visit. Typical scuba dive charges internationally attract a US$25 supplement. VAT on a typical upscale hotel room generates US$40 a night. A typical visitor on a one week dive vacation can thus generate almost US$500 in direct revenues; about 500 such visitors a month would entirely finance the Fund requirements. Putting this into perspective, Tanzania typically received over 500 000 tourists annually from 2000 to 2003.

- Fisheries. Offshore fisheries in the EEZ are poorly regulated and much of the catch and effort is unreported. Based on reported statistics, however, the landed value of marine fisheries was approximately US$35 million in 2002; actual values could have been an order of magnitude higher. This suggests that, in a properly monitored and regulated fishery, a royalty of as little as 1 percent on fishery products may be adequate to cover the Fund inflow requirements.

- Oil and gas. Tanzania's offshore potential is not yet fully exploited, but the 270 MW potential power generation being provided by the Songo Songo gas field project provides a useful estimating basis. Electricity will have an average production cost of about US$0.07/kWh during the project life. If inflows to the Marine Legacy Fund were entirely financed through mechanisms that were included within the cost of power, the impact would be a US$0.0013/kWh on average production cost: a 1.8 percent increase.

- Other. Other potential sources of funding also remain available. The Marine Legacy Fund remains the natural repository for capital endowments or donations from foreign donors, private foundations, or the sale and lease of select island properties.

In short, relying on such financial inflows is not unreasonable. A mix of tourism, fisheries, and nonrenewable offshore resource income could adequately finance such a scheme. So, is it financially feasible? The answer is "Yes." Is it institutionally feasible? That we will need to revisit in the next chapter.

Financial Endpoint

We started this chapter on financial sustainability by talking about a permanent income, and the financial endpoint in Blueprint 2050 would, in effect, see a permanent income in place for each community, for each MPA or MMA, for each local network, and for the system as a whole. Under Blueprint 2050, each MPA or MMA would use best available mechanisms to reduce costs and maximize revenues locally, sharing these burdens and benefits according to protocols established through co-management agreements. Those areas that generate routine surpluses pay partially into a common funding pool of about US$50 million – we call this a Marine Legacy Fund. Those areas of national priority that require subsidy can draw from this funding pool. The revolving nature of the Marine Legacy Fund is intended to provide adequate buffer for periodic shocks (such as revenue shortfalls or emergency expenditures), while also taking advantage of replenishment through other sources, such as routine budget allocations, revenue shares from offshore fishery rents, royalty shares from offshore mineral, oil or gas development, selected fines and levies, and potential external assistance or budget support. In getting to this point of having a guaranteed permanent income, we may even end up selling off, or leasing, one or two of those smaller fascinating offshore islands. Oscar Wilde would be proud; as he too noted, "It is better to have a permanent income than to be fascinating."

INSTITUTIONAL ROBUSTNESS

Mvuvi anajua poweza alipo

The people's good is the highest law.

Cicero (106 BC - 43 BC),
De Legibus

Introduction

Up until about 15 years ago, most understood the idea of *"sustainable development"* to mean something to do with environmental quality, social equity, and economic efficiency. It is only in the past decade or so that we have gained a greater appreciation for the need for *institutional sustainability* as part of the overall equation. For a brief period in some places, that was interpreted as an excuse for building large institutions. The unsustainability of such institutions soon became evident. First, they often suffered from a lack of financial sustainability, as discussed in the previous chapter. But, more significantly, they often became too self-serving and inflexible: not responding to the needs of the people they were meant to serve. Consequently, the pendulum has started to swing the other way. We now have a

more moderated understanding that institutions, like ecosystems and human systems, need to be flexible and adaptive. We can better tolerate changes in our institutional structures. We understand that duplication or redundancy can at times be important as a safety net. We know that institutions often follow public requirements in a demand-driven response, rather than try to lead public needs through a more supply-driven approach. We know that small local institutions are as important as large national level ones. Institutions can and do interact and co-exist with the same degree of flexibility and complexity as individuals. Blueprint 2050 recognizes the need for and inevitability of such institutional structures.

But this greater flexibility should not be interpreted as greater uncertainty or fuzziness. Clarity remains important, and modern institutional structures –

Photo Paavo Eliste

including the laws, regulations, memorandums of understanding, and other instruments that govern their behavior – still have some rules. What is changing is that the rules are less prescriptive, and more descriptive. Rather than prescribing outcomes, they describe processes. They attempt to facilitate rather than regulate. There is greater *"devolution";* meaning that there may be general rules at one level about how rules should be made at a lower level. Tanzania is seeing this first-hand with the decentralization of government.

This chapter focuses on what we call institutional robustness. We see this as a way of regarding institutional structures – that include organizations, networks of organization, rules, laws, regulations, and any associated protocols – within a dynamic and complex structure. Essentially, we see the institutions inside a marine management system as flexible entities that respond effectively to outside forces and ongoing internal management needs. More specifically, we see the institutional structures as a complex web of different nodes that are themselves dynamic; working in many ways as the human nervous system and brain. Nodes may become more or less active; some may die or lie dormant. Some may duplicate the work of others. In using this metaphor, we can focus on a few simple questions.

First, is the current structure adequate? This first question is answered by a comprehensive review of existing structures. The conclusion is quite simply that, by and large, the system is adequate with most of the key elements in place.

Second, we ask whether there are any serious duplications that may lead to inconsistencies. In effect, we acknowledge that redundancy is fine, but are more concerned if redundancy may lead to ambiguity through lack of harmonization. We argue that harmonization of goals is necessary (and currently evident) but that harmonization of instruments among different jurisdictions is less critical. Specifically, we acknowledge that Zanzibar islands and mainland Tanzania can have quite different ways of approaching similar management issues. Furthermore, individual networks – or MPAs and MMAs within networks – can have different approaches depending on the local needs.

Third, we consider whether there are any serious gaps in the system. These would be the first line priority for fulfilling the institutional needs of Blueprint 2050. The main gaps relate to traditional use rights and to enforcement authority. Existing legislation provides inadequate recognition and attention to traditional use rights; co-managed local areas will require strengthening of legislation to make arrangements clear and protect traditional interests. Also, enforcement authority and responsibility in a decentralized context often lacks clarity in existing institutional and legal frameworks; this is often tied to the inadequate basis for zonation within MPAs or other managed areas. Finally, transboundary issues are currently not well coordinated and require strengthened regional institutions.

In closing, we take a closer and more practical look at co-management, and what that would entail in practice from a legal and institutional perspective. We propose that an important enabling link would be the establishment of District or Municipal Waters – in effect a *"Community Territorial Sea"* – lying wholly within the territorial seas but not less than 3 nautical miles from shore as an outer limit.

Point of Departure

Introduction

Although Tanzania is a unitary state, composed of Tanzania mainland and Zanzibar, the two sides of the Union have discrete legal systems and governmental and legislative structures. The Constitution of the United Republic of Tanzania promulgated in 1977 prescribes in its First Schedule a list of *"Union Matters."* Marine and fisheries are not one of those Union matters. Because marine and fisheries matters are non-Union matters, Zanzibar has a discrete legal regime for protection of marine resources.

Marine conservation initiatives in Tanzania are rather a recent phenomenon. The first areas were declared marine reserves in 1975 under the Fisheries Act of 1970. In 1988 Zanzibar adopted its own Fisheries Act, which is also used to establish marine protected areas. Tanzania mainland and Zanzibar share the same EEZ as prescribed under international law.

Policies, Statutes and International Legal Instruments in the URT and Zanzibar.

A wide range of laws are of potential relevance to the protection or conservation of marine ecosystems.

Policies

Fisheries Policy and Strategy, 1997

National Integrated Coastal Environment Management Strategy, 2003

National Environmental Policy, 1997

Tanzania State of the Coast, People and the Environment, 2001

The National Poverty Eradication Strategy, 1998

The Poverty Reduction Strategy Paper, 2000

Statutes

Constitution of the United Republic of Tanzania, 1977

Deep Sea Fishing Authority Act, 1998

District and Town Council Act (Zanzibar)

Environmental Management for Sustainable Development Act, 1996 (Zanzibar)

Fisheries Act, 1970, 2003 (revised)

Fisheries (Principal) Regulations, 1989

Fisheries (Prohibition of use of specified vessels or tools) Regulations, 1994

Forest Act, 2002

Forest Resources Management Act, 1996 (Zanzibar)

Geza Village Environmental Conservation Bylaws, 2002

Land Tenure (Village Settlement) Act, 1965

Local Government (District Authorities) Act, 1982

Local Government (Amendment) Act, 1999

Marine Parks and Reserves Act, 1994

Mining Act, 1998

National Parks Ordinance, 1959

Public Service Act, 2002

Territorial Sea and Exclusive Economic Zone Act, 1989

Town and Country Planning (Public Beaches) Regulations, 1992

Village Land Act, 1999

Wildlife Conservation Act, 1974

Zanzibar Fisheries Act, 1988

Zanzibar Fisheries Regulations, 1993

International Legal Instruments

Convention on Biological Diversity, 1992 [ratified 1996]

Convention on International Trade in Endangered Species, 1975 [ratified 1979]

UN Convention on the Law of the Sea, 1982 [ratified 1985]

Ramsar Convention on Wetlands of International Importance, 1971 [ratified 2000]

UNEP Convention for the Protection, Management and Development of the Marine and Coastal Environment of Eastern African Region, 1985

World Heritage Convention, 1975 [ratified 1977]

Marine protected areas were addressed by the mainland Tanzania government by enacting the Marine Parks and Reserves Act (MPRA) of 1994, which provides for the establishment, management and monitoring of marine parks and marine reserves, and the institutional framework for their management. The MPRA emphasizes community involvement in its legislation and has been generally well received. In Zanzibar, management of most marine areas falls under the jurisdiction of the Fisheries Division of the Ministry of Agriculture, Natural Resources, Environment and Co-operatives (MANREC). The management of Zanzibar's national parks falls to the National Protected Areas Board under the 1996 Environmental Management for Sustainable Development Act.

MPA and Fisheries Legislation In Tanzania

Fisheries legislation in Tanzania has been recently overhauled, with a new Bill before parliament in 2003 intended to replace the 1970 Fisheries Act. MPA legislation of 1994 designates the Division of Fisheries – which contains the Marine Parks and Reserves Unit – as the responsible agency for MPAs in mainland Tanzania.

The institutional framework for management of fisheries resources under the new Act is largely unchanged. The Director of Fisheries is the statutory officer in charge of fisheries management. The Director is empowered under the Act to appoint officers for purposes of licensing fishing activities and registering fishing vessels, enforcement of fisheries laws, and inspection of fishing activities.

The new Act provides for linkages among other sectors and the fisheries sector. The Act requires the Director to keep informed and consult local government authorities in the management of fisheries resources, and to reconcile any variance that may arise in the course of undertaking any management measures. The Director, however, retains regulatory powers in that he can intervene where the local authority does not exercise effective management of the resources. The Director may serve notices to the defaulting local government and can also seize fisheries management from such local authorities. While the Act does not detail the extent of the mandates of local authorities in fisheries management, it does indicate what should be done when a local authority does not exercise its *"fisheries management functions."*

MPAs are not explicitly addressed in the new Act, although Section 17(h) provides that the Minister of Natural Resources and Tourism may adopt measures *"prohibiting fishing in designated areas"* and that also the Minister may make regulations under Section 57(m) *"providing for the protection of critical habitats."*

An important new provision is the formal recognition of Beach Management Units (BMUs). While a common management instrument, BMUs are now formally defined to mean *"a group of devoted stakeholders in a fishing community whose main function is management, conservation and protection of fish in their locality in collaboration with the government."* To promote local fisheries, the Act gives powers to the Director to enter into management agreements with BMUs. The minimum contents of the agreements are provided under the Act.

Modern Marine Protection from Old Legislation.

Section 4 of Tanzania's 1970 Fisheries Act empowered the Minister responsible for fisheries management to make regulations which in his or her opinion were necessary or expedient for the sake of protecting, conserving, developing, regulating or controlling the capture, collection, gathering, manufacture, storage or marketing of fish and fish products.

Under this provision, the Minister could designate marine protected areas. For example the Order to close the Upangu, Katanga and Dambwe reefs was issued and gazetted under Section 4. The reefs are located in Tanga, Muheza and Pangani districts. These reefs are no-take zones; local government fisheries officers enforce the ban.

The key legislation dealing with MPAs on the mainland is the *Marine Parks and Reserves Act (MPRA)*. It establishes the Marine Parks and Reserves Unit (MPRU) and it provides for the *"establishment, management and monitoring of marine parks and reserves."* The principal functions of the MPRU are to establish and monitor control, management, and administration of marine parks and resources; and to raise funds for the establishment and development of marine parks and reserves, and to expend those funds accordingly. Other functions of the MPRU include enforcing and implementing the Act and its regulations, as well as conducting educational campaigns. In accordance with the Act, the MPRU Manager is answerable to both the Board of Trustees and the Director of Fisheries.

A Board of Trustees of Marine Parks and Reserves provides an advisory role to the Director and the MPRU, and is responsible for policies and oversight on the use by the MPRU of a Marine Parks and Reserves Revolving Fund. The Board also has a more direct role as it may instruct the MPRU Manager in the drafting and implementation of regulations, and on the designation of parks, reserves, and buffer zones in specified marine and coastal areas.

On the approval of the Board, each marine park has an advisory committee appointed by the Principal Secretary. The committees advise the Board on the management of the parks and provide oversight in the operation of the parks. The committees also consult with the wardens on day to day functions of the park. Local governments surrounding the park or reserve are members of the committee.

The Revolving Fund is made of government contributions, donations, and income from various businesses conducted or investments made by the parks or reserves. The MPRU manager may with the approval of the Board expend the funds in the following manner:

- Develop the marine park or reserve for any purpose relating to the functions of the MPRU.

- Apportion funds in accordance with the general management plan for the benefit of the villages in the vicinity of the park or reserve.

MPAs are Formed in Tanzania either through National or Local Instruments.

Nationally, marine parks are established by the Minister after consultation with the relevant local government authorities (including village councils) and by a resolution of Parliament. The declared area may be within territorial waters or in the EEZ or any coastal island or coastal area. The declaration may be in response to a national government initiative, or to requests made by individuals, research organizations, NGOs, the private sector or a local government authority. In establishing marine reserves the Minister does not need the resolution of the Parliament. Upon completion of the process, a Notice of the Declaration of an MPA is gazetted in the Government Gazette and becomes law.

Locally, the process is similar. Local authority may decide on its own initiative or through request from some other entity or individual to declare a marine protected area. The local authority designates and provides for management of MPAs under the Local Government Acts. Bylaws are prepared to give legal backing to the designation and management of the MPAs; these are in turn approved at different levels and become legally binding.

Photo: Paavo Eliste

● Apportion net revenue to local authorities in the marine park or reserve.

The MPRA stipulates the objectives of establishing a marine park or reserve to include conservation, protection, and restoration of: (a) the species and genetic diversity of living and non-living marine resources, and (b) the ecosystem processes of marine and coastal areas. It also includes the development and recovery of damaged areas, and the stimulation of rational utilization of under-utilized natural resources. In addition, another objective is to involve villagers and other local residents in all stages of managing the MPA, including the sharing of benefits associated with operating the protected area. Education and research goals are also embedded in the key objectives of establishing the protected areas.

The MPRA provides for formulation of General Management Plans (GMPs). The plans are supposed to be a guidance tool for the use and protection of resources in a marine park or reserve. The GMP provides a description of the nature and location of the area, its biological, environmental, geologic and cultural resources, its zoning, and the activities to be carried out in its buffer zones and submerged lands. The GMPs are prepared in close collaboration with the Planning Commission or any other regional planning body. Because GMPs are not gazetted, they are not binding; they are used primarily as a guiding tool for marine resource management.

The MPRA requires involvement of villages proximate to a marine park or reserve. The warden involves – formally or informally – such villages in the establishment of the MPA and in the preparation of the general management plan (GMP), zoning or amendment of regulations. These planning, zoning and regulatory instruments can apply to either the land or the sea. The village representative is also mandated under the Act to advise the technical committee, the MPRU Manager or the warden on any matters relevant to management and conservation of the marine park or reserve, and serves as a liaison between the village community and MPRU. Villagers must be notified of any decision or impending deliberations relating to the formulation or amendment of general management plans, regulations or zoning.

Another management control tool introduced by the MPRA is the requirement for an Environmental Impact Assessment (EIA) for certain activities to be carried out in marine parks. Construction and land allocations for development purposes are subjected to EIA. The EIA requirements are meant to supplement other controls stipulated under the Act such as GMPs and zoning. For instance, under Section 24(1) all commercial activities are prohibited unless specifically permitted under the GMP or regulations adopted for that marine park or reserve. Likewise restricted are activities that may impact marine parks or reserves or buffer zones and adjacent areas because of waste discharges. Similarly, the Act prohibits mining and installation of heavy industry within a marine park in a manner that may negatively impact the area through spillage of oil, chemical or other hazardous substances. Violations of these restrictions are criminalized under the Act.

While there may appear to be many facets to the overall planning process, the typical steps taken are relatively straightforward. First, strategic environmental assessment (SEA) is used as a broad spatial planning tool that captures different management opportunities and constraints based on available resources and local development needs. The SEA in turn permits the demarcation of Special Area Management Plans (SAMP) for areas that are regarded as being particularly sensitive or in need of targeted management. The SAMP can then be used for more detailed zoning – of both the land and sea – with a view to defining permitted uses within such delineated zones, as well as the rights and responsibilities of various parties (including government) within these zones (such as monitoring or enforcement). Such detailed zoning could include different forms of protection within a marine protected area, or different co-management regimes within the territorial sea. At this stage, once a potential development project has been identified to take advantage of specific economic opportunities, an EIA may also be required to ensure that proper mitigation measures are put in place as part of the investment, and that the project is consistent with the overall management plan.

A key enforcement aspect of the MPRA prohibits consumptive uses of fisheries resources in or around a marine park or reserve. No person shall, except in accordance with the terms and conditions stipulated in the Act:

- Fish, hunt, kill or capture any fish or animal or disturb any egg, nest, roe, or spawn within the marine park or reserve.

- Gather, collect or remove any fish, animal, aquatic flora, vegetation, or the products thereof, or any sand, minerals, or aquatic substrate.

Further controls permit any authorized officer to:

- Arrest any person found committing an offence under the Act or its regulations.

- Board and search any vehicle or vessel or any part of a vehicle or vessel.

- Enter any premise or land to seize or remove any fish or aquatic flora.

Any offender or things seized in the commission of an offence under the Act have to be taken as soon as possible to the district magistrate's court. The court may fine or imprison any person who causes damage to "*any fish, animal, aquatic flora, subsurface formation or mineral*"; that person may also be required to pay for the value of or restoration of the damaged resources.

The Marine Parks and Reserves Act also extends application to the Wildlife Conservation Act and the National Parks Ordinance in as far as marine parks or marine reserves are concerned. But it does not incorporate the provisions of international conventions for the protection of the marine ecosystems, particularly the Convention on International Trade in Endangered Species (CITES).

Marine protection may also be afforded through *local government* instruments, as opposed to centralized instruments; various parts of the Land Tenure (Village Settlement) Act, the Village Land Act, and the Local Government Act (LGA) recognize the local mandate for resource management. For example, amendments made to the LGA in 1999 state that "*it shall be the duty of local authorities in performing their functions to provide for the protection and utilization of the environment for sustainable development.*"

Village Mandates for Environmental Management.

In Tanzania the lowest administrative unit of the local government ladder is the village council. Section 22 of the Local Government Act provides for the functions and mandates of a village council, which is a body corporate capable of suing and being sued. The said functions include: planning and coordinating the activities of, and rendering assistance and advice to, the residents of the village engaged in aquaculture, fishery, agriculture, horticultural forestry or other activity or industry of any kind; and to encourage the residents of the village to undertake and participate in communal enterprises. Village councils may also propose bylaws to be adopted by the village assembly before being approved by the district council.

Local governments are also responsible for licensing of artisanal fishing activities and enforcement of fisheries bylaws. They are responsible for revenue collection and proposing biodiversity conservation areas for gazetting as protected areas. In addition, they are in charge of managing village and/or local government forest reserves. They are also involved in overall management of marine parks/reserves, mostly through the advisory committees set by the Marine Parks and Reserves Act. The Act is relevant to the management of marine resources that are within the jurisdiction of local authorities.

MPA and Fisheries Legislation in Zanzibar

The modern provisions for MPA designation and management are captured in Zanzibar's *Environmental Management for Sustainable Development Act*. Zanzibar enacted this framework law to govern its environment and natural resources. A special committee on Environment of the Revolutionary Council administers the Act. The chair of the Committee is the Chief Minister or his designated Minister. The committee has advisory, adjudicatory and decision-making powers on issues relating to the environment in Zanzibar.

The Act requires that localized plans be prepared where localized environmental problems have been identified and may threaten Zanzibar's biological diversity or an ecosystem such as a coastal or water catchment area. Integrated coastal area management planning is regulated and provides that *"The Minister on recommendation from the Director, in collaboration with the responsible institutions and in consultation with the users of the coastal environment may ... declare one or more coastal areas for integrated multi-sectoral planning."* For an area to qualify for such a declaration it must be of definable geographical boundaries, be of significant environmental value, and include intensive human activity of significant economic and social value. The planning activity is then based on a survey that describes the coastal area and its boundaries, takes an inventory of the coastal environment, identifies uses of the area, and incorporates any other relevant matter. The Act requires integrated coastal area management plans to be prepared in consultation with other responsible institutions and be consistent with the goals of existing environmental action plans prepared at different levels. The coastal area management plans are also required to allocate the costs and benefits of the plan in an equitable manner.

The Act also introduces *"a national protected areas system"* comprising terrestrial, aquatic, and mixed territorial aquatic ecosystems. Existing reserves, sanctuaries, controlled areas, and any other areas protected wholly or in part by a lead institution are also included in the system. The objectives of establishing the national protected areas system are: preservation, sustainable utilization by residents in and near the protected area, development of genetic resources, education and research, and eco-tourism and recreation. In addition, the Act provides the criteria for recommending an area to be included in the national protected area system. The criteria may include: richness in biodiversity, uniqueness, international significance, species value, and representation within a variety of Zanzibar's ecosystems. The law allows any person to petition the institution responsible for protected areas to nominate an area for protection under the Act. The institution responsible for the national protected areas system is duty bound to prepare rules regulating access and permissible uses, and to prescribe zoning requirements for the national protected areas.

The Act gives significant powers to the Minister responsible for environment with regard to protected areas. The Minister is empowered under the Act to declare any area of Zanzibar (terrestrial, aquatic or mixed aquatic and terrestrial) to be an area of international significance under international agreements. Under the Act, it is only the President who is empowered to remove an area from a national protected area system. The President would do so only after a recommendation from the institution responsible for protected areas, and prior approval of the Committee based on a completed EIA.

The law declares that the National Protected Areas Board shall be the institution responsible for the national protected areas system. The Board formulates and coordinates government policies on protected areas; it approves management plans for protected areas; and it may also recommend to the Minister areas that are suitable to be declared as protected areas. The Board may designate one or more leading institutions or qualified persons as the management authority of a national protected area. The authority has the task of managing the protected area and preparing a management plan in accordance with the Act. The plan is legally binding after being gazetted in accordance with the Act.

The law also establishes the National Fund for Protected Areas, which may be used for purposes of protecting, enhancing, and managing the national protected areas system in Zanzibar.

In addition to the framework law, *Zanzibar's fisheries legislation* (Fisheries Act 1988 and associated regulations of 1993) has been historically important in MPA development. The Zanzibar Fisheries Act repealed certain laws related to fishing, and modernized provisions relating to the management and development of fisheries in the territorial waters of Zanzibar. The scope of the Act covers *"the territorial waters of Zanzibar and its exclusive economic zone."*

The Act stipulates that the Minister responsible for fisheries may, by order published in the Gazette, provide that no person shall engage in fishing or collection of fish, fish products and aquatic flora, without having obtained a license issued by the Director of Fisheries or an authorized officer. The Director may impose by order or as a condition in a license the following measures for proper management of fisheries resources:

- Closed seasons for designated areas, species of fish, or methods of fishing.

- Prohibited fishing areas for all or designated species of fish or methods of fishing.

- Establishment of territorial parks and sanctuaries for any purpose whatsoever.

Some marine protected areas have been declared under these provisions. For example, the Chumbe Island Coral Reef Sanctuary was declared in 1992 by the Zanzibar Government through an order in the Gazette based on Section 6(1) of the Act.

As on the mainland, the Minister may, by order published in the Gazette, *"declare any area or waters to be a controlled area in relation to all fish, fish products or aquatic flora, or in relation to any species or kind of fish, fish product or aquatic flora."*

The Zanzibar Fisheries Act also provides for the preparation and review of fisheries management plans. The plans must minimally include: the state of exploitation of each resource, its potential average and annual yields, the measures necessary to achieve its optimum utilization; and a determination of the amount of fish, if any, to be taken by foreign fishing vessels. The Act also makes provisions for protecting traditional fisheries against the industrial fisheries by undertaking *"such means as reserving areas for different kinds of fishing"* and also by giving preference to citizens in the issuance of fishing licenses.

The Minister may make regulations under the Act to protect spawning areas, to determine closed areas or periods, to prescribe fish landing areas and the management of such areas, and to promote and regulate cultivation of fish and territorial parks.

The Director is also empowered by the Regulations to take specific protective measures. It is an offence under the Regulations to use beach seine, to use explosives or poison, or to possess fish killed by explosives or poison. Destruction of spawning areas is an offence, as is water pollution. Removal of corals from the reefs is also prohibited under the Regulations.

Authorized officers have powers: to stop and board any vessel used in fishing or any vehicle used in transporting fish; to examine or take copies of licenses or log books or other documents; to examine fishing gear; to take samples of fish; to enter and search any premises not being used as a dwelling place; to arrest any person believed to have committed an offence under the Act; and to seize any fish, fishing gear, or vehicle used in the commission of the offence.

Zanzibar is also proposing an amendment to the 1988 Fisheries Act. The Zanzibar Fisheries (Amendment) Act 2003 replaces the term *"territorial park"* with *"controlled area."* The latter is defined under the amending Act to mean *"any marine or fresh water area declared to be a park, reserve, sanctuary, natural conservation area, or any area declared to be conservation area under this Act ... ."*

In the event an area is declared to be a controlled area, the amending Act provides that the Director shall prepare the following:

- Environmental impact assessment for the area.

- Management plan for the area.

- Socio-economic impact assessment.

- Management agreements with other responsible government institutions, the local community, and any private investor or NGO wishing to manage the area.

The amending Act provides further for the establishment of a Marine Conservation Unit (MCU) by the Minister upon receiving the advice of the Director. The Director shall, upon the establishment of the MCU, appoint staff to execute its duties.

Although the amending Act tries to introduce an institutional framework for the management of marine protected areas in Zanzibar, it does not specify clear mandates for the MCU; it also does not clearly lay out guidelines for zoning, regulation of access, and benefit sharing with the surrounding villages.

Legislation Respecting the EEZ

There are two key instruments dealing with the EEZ that apply both to the mainland and to Zanzibar: (i) Territorial Sea and Exclusive Economic Zone Act of 1989; and, (ii) Deep Sea Fishing Authority Act of 1998.

Tanzania enacted the *Territorial Sea and Exclusive Economic Zone Act* to, among other things, implement the UN Convention on the Law of the Sea (UNCLOS). The Act – which also applies to Zanzibar – is an *"Act to provide for the implementation of the Law of the Sea Convention … and in the exercise of the sovereign rights of the United Republic to make provisions for conservation and management, of the resources of the sea … ."* Under the Act, the Minister for Foreign Affairs may make regulations for *"conservation measures to protect the living resources of the sea."* The Act therefore creates another legal avenue for creation of marine protected areas especially within the EEZ. But most of the Act gives priority to the utilization of marine resources rather than to their protection or conservation.

Tanzania uses the Act to vest itself with sovereign rights over the EEZ, which includes rights to explore, exploit, conserve, and manage the natural resources, whether living or non-living, and rights to any economic activity in the EEZ. The wording also gives jurisdiction to Tanzania to ensure *"the protection and preservation of the marine environment"* in accordance with Article 56(1)(b) of UNCLOS. Under the Convention, countries can control fishing, bottom trawling, mining and other uses in the EEZ. But if a country does not make optimal use of its EEZ it is obliged under the Convention to open the area for other countries to use. It has been argued elsewhere that these provisions should be a powerful incentive for coastal states that have ratified the Convention to create MPAs in the EEZ.

Uncertainties remain under the Act. For example, it is unclear how the Ministry of Foreign Affairs will coordinate or link with the Ministry of Natural Resources and Tourism in the management of marine resources in the EEZ. Also, some provisions of the Act – such as fines and enforcement – go beyond that contemplated in UNCLOS.

The powers of enforcing the provisions of the Act are vested in *"authorized officers."* These officers have been described under the Act to include: fisheries officers of the government ministries responsible for fisheries; members of the defense and police forces; officers of the customs and sales tax department; the special force designated to prevent illegal trade in Zanzibar; and any other person approved by the minister for foreign affairs. Authorized officers have a range of powers including powers to search, board and seize vessels; to detain suspects; and to sell fish that has been seized.

The management of fisheries resources in the EEZ is in principle regulated under the *Deep Sea Fishing Authority Act* of 1998. The Act was enacted for purposes of regulating the deep sea in the EEZ and is to be *"construed as being in addition to and not in derogation of the Territorial Sea and Exclusive Economic Zone Act and shall for all intents and purposes complement that Act."* The Act applies to Tanzania mainland and Zanzibar but it is not yet operational, as the Minister has not appointed the date of its coming into operation as required by Section 1 of the Act. Even if it were to become operational, the Act does not make any reference to MPAs in the EEZ nor does it provide for any marine conservation mandates that should be exercised by the Authority.

The Deep Sea Fishing Authority (DSFA) established under the Act is intended to work through different bodies: executive, advisory, and management committees. The functions of the Authority are: to promote, regulate and control fishing in the EEZ of the United Republic; to regulate licensing of persons and vessels intending to fish in the EEZ; to initiate, implement and ascertain the enforcement of policies on deep sea fishing vessels; to formulate and coordinate programs for scientific research in respect of fishing; to formulate fisheries policies; and, to negotiate and enter into any fishing or other contract, agreement or any kind of fishing cooperation with any government, international organization or other institution in pursuance of the provisions of the Act.

Delays in implementing the Act are largely linked to difficulties associated with structural and functional issues. Structural issues relate to the way the DSFA will depend on other institutions to implement its monitoring and surveillance mandates. There is no *"system of collaboration"* that has been defined in the Act. Officials of those institutions mentioned under the Act are not recognized under the Act as *"authorized officers."* Functional issues arise because the Act does not specify clearly, and in detail, the extent of power that may be exercised by enforcers of the Act. In addition the DSFA has been given the mandate of outlining national policies on fisheries, which is a function of ministers responsible for fisheries on both sides of the Union.

Summary

The laws and policies in the URT and Zanzibar are relatively comprehensive. They permit establishment and management of marine protected areas, establishment of such areas through local government instruments, and management of these areas using a variety of mechanisms. Provisions exist for addressing the entire EEZ, for using revolving funds, and for applying regulatory and planning mechanisms such as EIA to link to other sector activities. In short, the core legal and institutional structure for effective MPA management is in place. But duplication and gaps remain; we look at some of these in greater detail in the following sections.

Harmonization

The issue of harmonization is often of interest to those involved in trade or joint management. Harmonization can provide a common understanding of goals and of management methods; a common framework can provide greater administrative efficiency, and fewer disputes during implementation of monitoring and enforcement programs. In MPA management, it makes sense to have compatible definitions of what is – in fact – an MPA. Harmonization is also of relevance in situations where two parties are trading something, or are both trading to a common third party. For example, if both Zanzibar and Tanzania are issuing fishing licenses to foreign fleets, harmonization is of interest because otherwise they may end up competing to the point that fewer rents are captured by both parties.

But international experience also tells us that full harmonization is not always possible, nor is it always necessary. The Organization of Eastern Caribbean States attempted for over a decade to harmonize and standardize all of its environmental legislation; the current situation is that all of the States have their own laws, which look quite different, but which all have compatible and complementary goals. Harmonization of objectives has occurred, even though the methods may differ. In trade, as well, the early literature emphasized the necessity of common trade and environmental practices to prevent the creation of pollution havens, but we now know from analyses of circumstances within large trading blocks (such as North America or Europe) that *"unharmonized"* instruments do not generally lead to the presumed distortions. What we have learned from all of this experience is that harmonization of goals is more critical than harmonization of specific instruments. Differences in legislation, in implementing institutions, or even in administrative procedures can still be compatible.

In the case of URT, some analysts have called for *"better harmonization"* of the Tanzanian and Zanzibar legal frameworks, institutions and definitions. This is often based on the presumption that a single framework is inherently better, or that a single institutional arrangement will be inherently better. We here consider three specific issues: implementing institutions, MPA definitions, and fishery legislation.

At an institutional level, there is currently no single strict harmonized framework that can facilitate joint management of marine protected areas between the mainland and Zanzibar. The Ministry of Agriculture, Livestock and Natural Resources deals with the establishment and management of conservation areas in Zanzibar while the same function is being done by the Ministry of Natural Resources and Tourism in the mainland. But in a system of networks such as that envisioned in Blueprint 2050, we do not, in fact, require a single strict harmonized framework. By the same token that we do not necessarily need identical structures within all MPAs or MMAs in Zanzibar or the mainland, there is no reason to believe that we need identical structures throughout the entire system. Experience elsewhere has shown that much can be accomplished with memorandums of understanding, and that these are often more amenable to change in an adaptive management structure.

A second case relates to the definition of MPAs. There is no single strict definition of an MPA in either Zanzibar or the mainland, and different statutes can now in fact be used to afford some form of protection to different parts of the marine ecosystem. Some have observed that *"we seem to have a legal situation where both Tanzania (sic) and Zanzibar may declare protected areas independently, and where there is no legal terminology that is binding for both parts of the Union."* Is this a serious situation requiring substantial reforms before we can move forward? We think not. The differences have themselves evolved to meet the needs of different circumstances. While it may be possible to harmonize and streamline some of these laws and definitions, at this point it is clear that the goals of the various pieces legislation are largely compatible (see Chapter 1 comparing some of the Zanzibar and Tanzania MPA goals).

The third area relates to fishery management in the EEZ. Both the URT and Zanzibar refer to *"their"* EEZ, while in fact UNCLOS states that a country can have only one EEZ. Some therefore question the international acceptability of the URT legislation. We assert that while there may be different internal claims, there is for international legal purposes only a single EEZ that relates to the URT and that claim does not involve any disputed territories. The issues are thus primarily domestic in nature, rather than international. There is little doubt that domestic issues are substantial, but they relate more to an issue of cooperation rather than harmonization. The two laws provide a good basis for cooperation between the two sides of the Union in matters relating to protection of marine areas, but so far their implementation has not been easy. The bone of contention between the two sides of the Union on marine issues is the interpretation of the Union Matters as contained in the Articles of the Union, which is one of the schedules of the 1977 URT Constitution. Officials in Zanzibar generally contend that fisheries and

Photo Dean Housden

marine conservation are non-Union matters; it is thus unconstitutional to try to bring those matters within the ambit of the Union. On the other hand, officials in the mainland contend that the EEZ is a Union matter (because it was established pursuant to an international convention) and therefore the two sides must cooperate to conserve the resources therein. Although fisheries is not a Union matter, the two sides of the Union do share the same EEZ and territorial sea and there is a mutual interest for cooperation for better management of the fisheries and other marine resources. Any inability to agree on the way forward impinges on conservation efforts for marine resources in the EEZ. There are mechanisms to resolve such issues. The Vice Presidents' Office on the mainland and the office of the Chief Minister of Zanzibar are responsible for dealing with the areas of cooperation and Union matters. One potential area of common ground is to establish a deep sea MPA in the EEZ, bringing together the two sides of the Union to cooperate and identify institutional modalities for governance of the MPA to promote mutual conservation goals. It could lead the way for cooperation of the parties in the larger issue of fisheries management in the EEZ.

Gaps

Blueprint 2050 argues that decentralized management within a system of networks is an effective way forward. To implement effective decentralized management, however, certain legislative gaps do need to be addressed in some fashion. These relate primarily to traditional use rights, enforcement in a decentralized context, and zonation in a decentralized context. Also, effective treatment of transboundary concerns remains an issue; but this issue is not confined only to Tanzania.

Traditional use rights

In some marine areas along the coast there are traditional or customary usage rights practiced by coastal communities. In some areas, communities have customary laws and practices that bestow them with ownership rights that exclude outsiders. Because these practices were established over the years, they are critical considerations that need to be reflected in the law to encourage better management, and

voluntary enforcement of the laws. Customary laws or practices, if consistent with MPA laws, may also form the basis for community support for MPAs.

Currently the fisheries laws and the Marine Parks and Reserves Act do not make provisions for recognition of customary laws and practices. This is one of the gaps in the legislation that needs to be addressed. Even in cases where customary practices conflict with the objectives of the MPA laws, awareness and enforcement efforts may help to change the existing practice.

Enforcement in a decentralized context

Law is not an end in itself, it has to be implemented on the ground to be effective. Enforcement of MPA legislation is inadequate in most areas along the coastline. One of the inherent problems of law enforcement in Tanzania is the prosecution process, which tends to be time consuming and complex. While fisheries officers collect evidence, and make arrests, seizures and forfeitures, prosecution of the offences is done by police officers. Police officers often fail to connect the evidence with the law and hence fail to secure convictions in court. Because fisheries laws are not the conventional criminal laws with which the police are familiar, most police officers are less knowledgeable about fisheries legislation and hence fail to prepare comprehensive charge sheets. Offenders of fisheries legislation are often acquitted by courts because of ill prepared cases.

Problems with weak enforcement capacity are exacerbated when decentralization of efforts is unclear about jurisdiction. The laws that establish marine protected areas generally provide for MPAs at a national level to be managed by a centralized institution. There is no clarity as to how the management roles are decentralized to local levels. Enforcement is especially a concern because the seas are themselves not delineated or demarcated in any formal and consistent manner. The most important step in this regard will be in generating greater clarity of jurisdiction and responsibility. This can be done in co-management agreements but increased clarity can also come through the legal framework. We will discuss later the potential role of a *"Community Territorial Sea."*

Clarity is Needed at the Village Level.

Section 35 of the Zanzibar Environmental Management for Sustainable Development Act gives local communities a role in the management of natural resources close to them, but does not go further to provide guidance on how to implement that objective. Another law – the District and Town Council Act – provides for the establishment at the district level of a standing Committee responsible for the protection of Environment and Social Welfare. Similarly, this Act is silent at the local village (Sheha) level. The Sheha is responsible for all matters including law enforcement in his area and reports directly to the District Commissioner.

In the mainland, the Marine Parks and Reserves Act does not make specific statements about the role of local government, except to say that they should receive a share of net revenues and be represented on the Advisory Committee. The Act does not provide how local government structures will assume management responsibilities in the MPAs.

Zonation and planning in a decentralized context

The overall zonation issue is linked to enforcement, but is more closely tied to local government legislation. Land use planning is an important conservation tool, but planning is often absent. In most districts, land allocation decisions are made unilaterally without coordination with other departments of local government. In some areas, land surveys have not been carried out for years due to lack of finance and personnel; land development is then done indiscriminately. Unplanned settlements are evident along the coast and beaches, despite the threat of beach erosion.

While land based activities do not pose a significant threat to the coastal resources, there is still a need to address them, as they might be a threat in the near future. In Pangani, a number of developments (hotels and houses) were constructed very close to beach areas. This is contrary to the Town and Country Planning (Public Beaches) Regulations, which require developments to take place at least 60 m from the beach. Popular waterfront dining establishments in Dar es Salaam also, in fact, contravene these regulations. Development also occurs in inter-tidal zones despite these being ecologically sensitive lands for conservation.

A promising basis for addressing zoning and land use issues is through the National Integrated Coastal Environment Management Strategy 2003. This comprehensively provides useful linkages between environment and poverty, and strongly advocates an integrated and participatory approach to coastal zone management. It also addresses the MPA concept by providing that:

- *"An Integrated Coastal Management Unit, in collaboration with relevant authorities, shall identify critical coastal areas and areas of high biodiversity that should be included within existing or new protected area programs. Areas and their bounds will be identified through a consultative process that includes input from local and national government, NGOs and resource users … . The national coastal program shall work with the Board of Trustees and Marine Park and Reserves Unit to establish new marine protected areas (under the Marine Parks and Reserves Act) in areas with significant biodiversity and where local communities support the concept of a park."*

In addition, the policy provides that:

- *"… there is a potential for a system of marine parks to play a central rote within the nation's overall ICM strategy. Finally, there are local coral reef management initiatives in Tanga and elsewhere [e.g., Menai Bay] that provide promising models for critical habitat management."*

Photo Paavo Eliste

Zonation should also more accurately be regarded as a means for capturing or creating opportunities, rather than imposing restrictions. For example, some proposals for waterfront development in the Dar es Salaam area are controversial because they entail conversion of some of the mangroves which are important bird habitats. But there is no reason why such proposals could not take a more comprehensive approach: one that eliminates non-sustainable resource use near the foreshore, provides other employment opportunities, and contributes revenues to the protection of habitat elsewhere. Contractual arrangements and zoning could be formulated within the context of current policies to simultaneously promote development and conservation goals. Capturing such zonation opportunities requires capacity building within local government. Capacity to identify opportunities, to value property for its best use, to identify trade-offs, and to negotiate with potential developers and investors, remains very weak.

Transboundary issues

Tanzania is party to many international legal instruments relevant to the protection of marine and coastal ecosystems. But, as in most British ex-colonies, international treaties have no direct effect within the domestic legal order unless they are adopted under domestic law. In international legal parlance, treaties are not self-executing in these countries. This dualist stance characterizes Tanzanian treaty practice, and international conventions on marine and coastal resources are no exception. Referring to the principles and practices of English Common Law, the practice in Tanzania has been that the treaty is signed subject to ratification either by tabling it before the Cabinet or by a resolution adopted by the Parliament. This is

followed by incorporation of the treaty into a national law by enacting the relevant legislation.

Although Tanzania has signed and ratified many international conventions relevant to marine and coastal protection, it is only UNCLOS and CITES that have been followed by specific implementing legislation. The common approach for Tanzania has been to implement conservation treaties with a general implementing legislation. An example of such a case is the Marine Parks and Reserves Act, which does not say which treaty or treaties it purports to implement. In cases where implementing legislation has been enacted, the provisions of such legislation have tended to be a *"pick and choose"* exercise from a broad range of provisions of a particular treaty. An example is the Territorial Sea and Exclusive Economic Zone Act which implements some but not all of the UNCLOS provisions; in this case the Act pays minimal attention to marine pollution that may heavily impact on a protected marine park or reserve in the Territorial Sea or EEZ.

Similarly, transboundary issues relating to marine parks have no formal home within Tanzanian legislation. This is not unusual in the regional context. The most significant sub-regional instrument of importance to the conservation of marine and coastal resources is the 1985 UNEP Convention for the Protection, Management and Development of the Marine and Coastal Environment of the Eastern African Region. Its related instruments are the Protocol Concerning Protected Areas and Wild Fauna and Flora in the Eastern African Region, and the Protocol Concerning Co-operation in Combating Marine Pollution in Cases of Emergency in the Eastern African Region. This Convention and its related protocols are not yet in force because the requisite minimum number of ratifications has not yet been reached. Tanzania is one of the State Parties that adopted the Convention but has not yet ratified it; as of 1992, only France, Kenya, and the Seychelles had ratified the Convention. This Convention is relevant to MPAs because its principal objective is to establish close cooperation to protect and improve the state of wild fauna and flora and natural habitats in the region by the establishment of specially protected areas in the marine and coastal environment.

Co-management Revisited – A Lawyer Speaks

Many of the tricky issues noted above seem somehow to be linked to issues over cooperative management. The Union issues between Zanzibar and Tanzania mainland require cooperative structures. Harmonization relies on cooperative arrangements. Resolution of traditional use rights needs to acknowledge different stakeholders. Local resource use planning, and subsequent enforcement, involves multiple stakeholders. Institutional robustness thus often reverts to some form of co-management, either through delegation of authority or through creation of new arrangements. The *"co-"* in co-management implies involvement of more than one party and legal concerns often come to the forefront. It thus seems prudent to turn to some legal opinion and advice at this stage.

From a legal perspective, what is co-management?

In its simplest terms, it is an agreement on how the rights and responsibilities associated with a resource are shared. It usually does not pertain to ownership. Ownership is usually not changed by such agreements, although resultant changes in rights might look like a change in ownership. If I own land and give you a 20 year lease, you might start behaving as if you owned it; but in fact I will still retain the property rights. How it is used at the expiry of the lease will be entirely up to me.

If ownership generally does not change, what is the point of a co-management agreement?

The point is to do something that makes sense for resource management. If you own or have a long lease on something, you are more likely to look after it in a way that it will still be useful to you in a few years, or in a few decades. It thus gives you more of an incentive. Also, if you are dealing with the resource on a day to day basis, while I as owner am living far away or know little about it, you can probably make more informed management decisions than I could. That aspect should make resource management more effective.

How is adaptive co-management different from simple co-management?

In principle it is also still an agreement. The main difference is that the agreement itself may not specifically define the rules of how rights and responsibilities are shared; instead the agreement only fixes the processes for defining and changing such rules. For example, a simple co-management agreement might say that I am in charge of monitoring, that you are in charge of enforcement, and that we share all costs and income 50-50. In an adaptive management agreement, we might state in addition that we will meet every three years to review these parameters and that we can at that time change them to reflect experience and then current conditions. Conditions can change – especially in environments of ecological, social or political uncertainty – so rules may need to change too. Obviously more complex ways and means are possible, but the spirit behind ACM is that ongoing learning and negotiations can strengthen and change the actual rules.

Who is normally involved with such agreements?

To answer this we should take a step back. It is helpful to think of two levels of agreement. The first level might be an agreement involving local players for a particular marine area. That might be a private sector operator, local government, and a local community group; let's call this threesome the *"local collective."* The second level might be an agreement between this local collective, and one or more non-local groups, such as national government through a ministry or some other larger government body. Two agreements could coexist: one governs how responsibilities and rights are split between national and local authorities; a second governs how the local rights and responsibilities are split among local stakeholders.

Let us be more specific then: Who might normally be involved with such co-management agreements at a national level?

In the current system, there is somewhat of a gap here. For marine parks, it is clear that the Division of Fisheries is the responsible institution on the mainland and that the Fisheries Department and the National Protected Areas Board are the responsible institutions on Zanzibar. For the EEZ, the Ministry of Foreign Affairs is the responsible institution, but there is no organization entrusted with day to day oversight of the EEZ. There has been a proposal put forward to establish a Deep Sea Fishing Authority – the DSFA – to take over government responsibilities relating to the EEZ. There is also a need for some coordinating mechanism if revenue sharing is instituted between networks, such as that contemplated in Blueprint 2050. The DSFA could potentially fulfill this function.

Is the DSFA the best institution to do this?

There is no best or worst institution. The main point in modern co-management agreements is to permit some flexibility so that, if conditions change, institutional arrangements will adapt accordingly. Whether it is the DSFA or some other body, the actual responsibilities and rights at stake will be the same; so the complexity of, and processes for, defining an agreement will be largely independent of which institutions are involved. My personal advice would be to focus first on defining the processes that identify those rights, responsibilities, and desired outcomes rather than on the actual institutions involved. Experience elsewhere shows that the most capable institution or institutions will often emerge from such processes.

At the local level, are there any pressing legal requirements before we can implement relevant structures?

Locally there are fewer issues of *"who"* but more issues of *"how."* Tanzania's legislation provides for increased jurisdictional control by districts, villages, and other local institutions. But the problem remains that marine resources are all in the sea, while most of the experience and legislation deals with terrestrial resources. We have a Forest Act, we have a Land Tenure Act, we have a Village Land Act. But we have no similar legislation for communal seas. Sure, we have legislation which says in principle the local authorities can manage some of these water resources, but it remains rather vague. Defining a *"community marine area"* is thus one of the most pressing legal requirements.

But I thought that any community could already do that, either directly or through petitioning national authorities for such gazetting. Is that not what you mean?

That is only part of the picture. The problem with that process is that it favors those communities that have strong institutions to begin with. Weaker communities may never be in a position to push their own interests or they may do so only very slowly. In the meantime, the resource continues to degrade. A more proactive policy or legal stance is required in such instances.

How have other countries addressed this issue? Are there any precedents?

Some countries have made significant headway by legislating a *"community zone"* within their territorial seas. In the Philippines, the community sea – it is legally called *"municipal waters"* – extended initially 7 km but was subsequently enlarged to 15 km from the shoreline. Indonesia has been considering legislation that places the historical 3 nautical mile territorial sea within the primary control of coastal communities.

It seems to me that such a proposal would require major changes to the legislation in Tanzania. Is it possible to introduce new instruments of that sort within the current context?

It might be new, but it is not necessarily such a drastic change. I believe that it is possible. First, Tanzania's near shore areas remain relatively unregulated and introducing something of this sort will not create any conflicting claims. Second, existing legislation would permit designation of such a near shore zone. Third, the new legislation that designates Beach Management Units provides a natural starting point. We would just need to agree on how far out such a community zone should or could be. But frankly, it is less material whether it is three, five, seven, nine or fifteen kilometers; the main point is that designating such a zone gives the coastal communities some certainty over their resource base. Many of the current uncertainties in Tanzania's legislation – over traditional use rights, over revenue sharing, over enforcement responsibility – would also be easier to address within such a designated community zone.

But then the communities would suddenly have a huge responsibility. Are they ready for it?

That is the beauty of adaptive co-management. This is not a windfall gain for these communities. We are simply acknowledging that there is a specific well-defined marine area that will continue to be co-managed by various stakeholders. National, district and village authorities will all have an ongoing role to play. Depending on local capacity, site to site management regimes can be different and can adapt as circumstances change.

Institutional Endpoint

Modern maritime law owes much to Hugo Grotius who, in 1605, made a case for why the Dutch should have uncontested access to maritime trade with the East Indies. In his *Mare Liberum* (Freedom of the Seas), Grotius argued that the Portuguese, and Spanish, were wrong in their exclusive claims to the entire oceans and to navigation rights over them. He argued, among other things, that a coastal nation could not claim sovereignty over the seas beyond the range of its control from shore. With time, this sovereignty claim translated into what was later called the *"cannon shot rule"*, and formed the basis for a 3 nautical mile limit that became the norm for British colonial near shore claims. Other countries followed suit. The 1982 Convention on the Law of the Sea, which has been called the modern Constitution for the Oceans, now recognizes the rights of coastal states to claim up to a 12 nautical mile territorial sea and an Exclusive Economic Zone up to 200 nautical miles.

Tanzania's and Zanzibar's system of legislation and institutions – while far from perfect – provides a reasonably sound basis for moving forward with the Blueprint 2050 Vision within all of its sovereign maritime territory. In previous chapters, we have argued the technical merits of establishing a system of networks to achieve ecological goals, of relying on adaptive co-management to help alleviate poverty, and of establishing funds to diversify risk and achieve financial sustainability. All of these technical needs can be catered for under existing mechanisms. Legislation permits establishment of MPAs, management of other marine areas, establishment of revolving funds, and involvement of community stakeholders. Planning mechanisms to address development needs through other economic activities can be similarly addressed through integrated planning mechanisms. Our endpoint for 2050 is thus not much different from our starting point of today, albeit regulations may be better harmonized, enforcement authority may be clearer, and more coastal people will have been involved in local participatory processes. But everything that we will see in fifty years will also be recognizable in today's policies, legislation, and other writings.

The one novel element will be that coastal communities will have primary control and access to the first three nautical miles of near shore seas. Or perhaps it will be nine nautical miles; perhaps it will be something in between. But the main point is that access will be well established within institutions and laws that respect such common local access, without the need to fire any cannons. While the *"cannon shot rule"* may be attributed to Grotius, he hoped that reasonable people would never need to revert to such methods.

The Roman people could not forbid any one from having access to the seashore, and from spreading his nets there to dry, and from doing other things which all men long ago decided were always permissible.

Celsus as quoted by: Hugo Grotius, 1605, Mare Liberum

FULFILLING EXPECTATIONS

Penye wengi hapaharibiki neno.

Ukiona vyaelea vimeundwa.

[When you see vessels afloat, somebody made them]

Zanzibari saying.

Actions speak louder than words. URT has an impressive record recently in translating visions into definite government policy actions. Even when positive consequences of such actions are not always clear or guarantied, the need to do something has always prevailed. When poverty remains high and fragile resources remain under constant threat, inaction typically makes things worse.

This book has laid out a broad vision for a system of networks; seven core priority networks are complemented by the sustainable management of an eighth network that comprises the EEZ. If successful, Blueprint 2050 will see 40 percent of the territorial seas protected through these core priority networks. Poverty will have been effectively eliminated in coastal areas, with local inhabitants participating meaningfully in local resource management decisions through adaptive co-management processes. The system itself will be financially sustainable, with the private sector playing an instrumental role in ensuring cost-effective management. External shocks – whether from political turmoil or climate change – will be mitigated by mechanisms that reduce the vulnerability of individual MPAs or networks; revenue sharing mechanisms at a national level will be based on a diversity of sources. A community-managed territorial sea will extend a few nautical miles from the shoreline; coastal communities will have primary responsibility for this area and their rights and obligations will be entrenched in law. Finally, institutional and legal mechanisms will adopt an adaptive stance that permits experimentation and evolution of the system. Just as ecosystems and humans adapt, we expect the system and individual networks to adapt as well.

As with any Vision, the first step in realizing it is for all to agree in principle that it is worth trying to achieve. This will require some dialog, but it will also require that people are willing to move forward with the spirit of discovery. As we said at the outset of the book, Blueprint 2050 is not so much a template as it is a process of building something. The adaptive processes that are espoused in this book permit changes in direction along the way; they permit experimentation, learning, and back-tracking. Unlike some other traditional system plans, this one is more organic: just like the people and ecosystems that comprise it.

Once endorsed, the second main challenge will be to manage and then fulfill expectations. As we argued in Chapter 3, perceptions can be a pivotal element in the potential success or failure of any idea. If years go by without any progress, enthusiasm can wane. If fears are permitted to outweigh the hopes, then necessary experiments may never be pursued. Among the greatest fears are those associated with the very traditional – and at times valid – idea that environmental protection and economic development are incompatible. We have deliberately avoided such discussions in this book; the theoretical and applied literature is replete with examples that – more often than not – demonstrate how environmental and economic goals are compatible and complementary. Conflicts between tourists and fishers, between fishers and conservationists, between development concerns and conservation concerns, have been successfully mitigated all over the world and Tanzania also has its fair share of experience with such successes. There is no recipe for success in achieving "win-win" outcomes, but common elements include: (i) willingness to explore options and learn from them; (ii) openness and transparency in negotiation; and (iii) an understanding that stalemates are in fact long-term "lose-lose" situations. Processes of adaptive co-management embrace all of these ideas, which is why we believe that – if the Blueprint 2050 Vision is adopted – the feared conflicts between protection goals and development goals will never materialize.

But we are not naïve. The proper management of expectations can make or break a project, and we thus devote this last chapter to addressing some of the potential fears, concerns and hopes that have been expressed within the community. Specifically, we hold up a series of views from the broad stakeholder community in Tanzania and Zanzibar, allowing them to propose their own solutions. Next, we review government commitment and steps taken to date that complement Blueprint 2050, concluding with some specific actions.

Managing Expectations – The Stakeholders Speak

The Blueprint 2050 Vision has had a considerable amount of stakeholder input from a wide cross-section of government and civil society. It would be impossible to record all of the positions in this book, but we can take some highlights from various conversations. Represented here are:

Bakari Asseid of DCCFF Zanzibar;

Jason Rubens from the WWF Seascape Program;

Jim Anderson and

Matt Richmond of Samaki Consultants;

Amani Ngusaru from the EAME Program;

Josephine Meela from the National Environmental Management Council;

R Mapunda who is Acting Director Fisheries;

CK Rumisha who is Head of MPRU; and

a dive shop owner from Zanzibar who wished to remain anonymous.

 A warm welcome to everybody.

Blueprint 2050 proposes a system of substantial size. Some 40 percent of the territorial seas would be managed in the core priority areas, and the entire EEZ would fall under some complementary management as an eighth network. Is it too large or too ambitious?

 The size of the EEZ and the coast will not change. We cannot run away from that fact. Moreover, the linkages between the parts are not just physical, they are also human. People live up and down the whole coastline, and depend on the entire EEZ.

 Yes, it is a realistic scale. It depends ultimately on how much you do in each place. But having a system in place for this scale is certainly doable. Including the EEZ is important. Deep seas protected areas are generally overlooked, and these should be more manageable since there are not the social issues that you need to deal with on land. Actually, it is high time to look at the EEZ, particularly the area beyond the near shore area. It is part of the deep water; science can and should be emphasized.

 An unfortunate reality of this scale is the wide dispersion of fishing effort. The system would be far more effective, of course, if there were adequate enforcement of existing rules and regulations.

Are there any priority areas within the proposed system? How can we resolve different ideas about priorities?

The Rufiji–Mafia–Kilwa complex is a real gem – a complex of uniqueness. It shows linkages of different ecosystems, with mangroves on the land side, and the delta and coral reefs in the near shore and offshore. Understanding the water flow is the key to all of this. Just look at any ocean current map: the equatorial currents hit the East African coast right at this point and nutrients flow in all directions from here. It is a regionally significant area.

What we need to keep in mind is that all of the areas can be important in the future, no matter what their present status. Even degraded areas can be addressed through restoration efforts; there is no reason to ignore them. An area such as Chwaka Bay, for example, can be completely restored in 50 years. A long time frame helps give this perspective.

It is difficult to prioritize ecology. Is reef more worthy than sea grass? I can't see why, if they are all interconnected. One thing about the areas identified in Blueprint 2050: each one covers a range of ecologies. Pemba has coral reef, of course, but it also has muddy embayments, sea grass beds, mangroves and coral rubble areas. I would not worry much about prioritizing between these areas based on ecological criteria; it may make more sense to look at the threats to each area in setting priorities.

And what about cultural assets? Modern definitions of MPAs seem to include cultural values, but are such values relevant to Tanzania?

The cultural value of some resources – archaeological sites, sacred rivers, caves, etc. – are important as tourism attractions as well as for getting support from local communities. These assets contribute to national income and, therefore, need to feature in the definition of MPAs; they also need to be conserved and protected to ensure that income accruing from them is sustainable.

Communities are seen as an important focal point in managing, or co-managing, their natural resources. But we have learned that perceptions of conflict might get in the way of sound management. Do you see a way forward through this?

Perceptions are often mis-perceptions. You can take the example of Jibondo. The village leader agreed to close the reef, and then there were protests. But protests went beyond the issue of reef closure. Protests were really about attempts by government to control individual freedoms. It is all about the freedom of action.

Another whole issue is the variability of communities. All communities are not the same. Some are traditionally anarchic, anti-management, anti-government. There are real differences between communities on the coast and we need to respect these. The Tanga approach would not work in Songo Songo without some modification. In this context, expectations for time frames are also unrealistic. There is an urgent need to capture the requirements of community-based MMA in legislation. For instance, the current requirement in the Act is that there must be a management plan in place within 6 months of gazetting; this is simply not realistic in a community managed area, and forcing such time frames will inevitably and unnecessarily lead to conflict. Flexible adaptive models are appropriate in such instances.

There are problems with every model, but co-management is the best model. It is the most cost effective. Initially you need a big investment in training, seminars, workshops and facilitation. The initial capital is heavy and also heavy in terms of time. But after that heavy investment, operational costs will be lower. Communities are all over the coast. They know what is going on, the people, who is doing what. When people realize they profit from the activity, they will control the activity very well.

Some claim that current laws do not adequately address customary rights and uses. Is it possible to entrench customary rights? Blueprint 2050 proposes the idea of a community territorial sea as a way forward. Is this a realistic idea?

The law is probably too strong in some areas. Regarding seine netting, for example, it may not be unsustainable in all places. We are missing some research to demonstrate that seine netting is really bad; the general law could be refined to have the ban only in certain areas and then leave local management to the coastal communities. The same goes for coral mining: districts should have the right to decide the limits. Renewable resource exploitation should be allowed with sustainable levels of harvesting.

In theory we can say that we should have legislation for customary rights. Zanzibar has some community based laws, but in practice we have a very long shoreline. To have a boundary in the water saying this belongs to this community and the adjacent is belonging to another community is not easy. When you go beyond the 12 mile zone it becomes even more difficult; even within this zone it cannot be entirely managed by communities. But giving some local control makes sense: perhaps a 5 km zone can be managed by communities. Outside 5 km you need more powerful boats, even helicopters.

How does scientific information factor into the planning process? Blueprint 2050 calls for a substantial effort in information gathering, and even proposes that Tanzania establish a national biogeographical classification system.

Science is critical. We need to know what we should protect and what is the importance of the area to the economics of the place... the livelihood potential. Ecological information, fisheries information, coral reef information: they are all important. The information should be there before we create parks.

Everybody can agree that we need better science to make better decisions. But there is a dilemma in this. Gathering information often takes time. During that time further degradation can happen and by the time you have decided to protect an area, it may no longer be worth protecting. An alternative more precautionary approach is to give everything some form of basic protection through gazetting or other means, then gather information, then degazette those areas that are less important.

A system of networks can be built using either approach. The traditional approach is to gazette based on science. The precautionary approach is to gazette everything and then degazette based on science. The costs are in fact not that much different, but with the precautionary approach you have to be willing to live with paper parks for a while and people need to understand the longer-term plan and the adaptive processes and mechanisms at work. Some countries – such as the Philippines – have used the precautionary approach with some success in the end. But it does require a commitment to adaptive planning.

Blueprint 2050 proposes a pooled fund – a Marine Legacy Fund – for pooling revenues and buffering against risks. Is this a reasonable approach?

I used to think that the greatest strength of the legislation is that revenues generated by one MPA stay with that MPA. I now understand the need for pooling and sharing of revenues. I understand that there cannot be 100 percent retention, but I still believe that there should be some level of retention to give some level of comfort to the management of the specific MPA and the participants; 70 percent retention may be good.

When revenues are higher, then you can afford to support the others. First you support the parts that are generating the revenues to ensure that these revenues are sustainable, then you can consider support to the others that are not generating revenues. You have to do a lot with the first one initially. We learned this lesson from our Lake Victoria experience.

There was earlier on an attempt to set up such a common fund but it was rejected because of inconsistencies in some of the legislation and some of the current institutional arrangements. But we have moved forward. We now have what we call a Fisheries Development Fund, for example, that can theoretically cater to many activities – including MPAs and research.

Blueprint 2050 foresees that the private sector will be an important stakeholder in future marine and coastal management. Is this a reasonable expectation?

The private sector has a lot to offer, most notably in the area of doing things cost efficiently. Government also is not very good at picking business opportunities; it is not set up to take that sort of risk and has no experience in it – that sort of risk should be left to private investors. But we should not rely on the private sector to realize all cost reductions or to do everything. The government will remain an important partner and will be part of much of the management; they should also strive to reduce their own costs where they can. The recent practice of paying government officials a sitting fee or a per diem to participate in meetings is an example; some projects may be able to afford that but ultimately it is an unsustainable practice and sets a bad precedent.

We must recognize that communities themselves form an important part of the "private sector." They are the ones that will be benefiting from their alternative income generation activities. But you need to be careful with such AIGAs. It is very hard to find something that works, is locally acceptable, and has available markets. I would put a focus on making existing activities more sustainable: help communities monitor and control outsider access; look into loan schemes for fishers; take a close look at agricultural activities. Do not forget that fishermen also farm: activities could include farming, tree planting, micro-credit for enterprises. The bottom line is that we should strengthen and promote activities that people are already doing, but we help them do it better.

Where do we start with any of these initiatives, many of which are interlinked? Blueprint 2050 is a long term vision but the first steps must start somewhere.

We must remember that we are not starting from square one. Tanzania already has broad experience with many of the issues identified here. Co-management has already been tested in places like Tanga and Menai. We have experience with tourism fees and licenses. Many lessons from terrestrial protected area management – through TANAPA, for example – can help inform marine protected area management. Our starting point is thus not so much a "point" – it is a range of activities and we will be able to move forward faster on some issues than on others. For instance, revenue and cost sharing arrangements might be put in place quickly in some parts of the coastal zone. By contrast, entrenching customary rights or organizing effective oil spill contingency plans will take longer.

A good place to start would be through the linkage between the Blueprint 2050 vision and the National Integrated Coastal Environment Management Strategy. The coastal management strategy can address issues relevant to management of components of the proposed system, and can suggest solutions and their implementation mechanisms. The strategy is therefore a useful reference tool for implementation of aspirations of the vision, within the five year time frame of the strategy.

Photo: Claudio Georgette

Priority Near-term Actions

Stakeholder views generally show that there is a willingness to find solutions to any problems that might arise in addressing a bold Vision such as that proposed in Blueprint 2050. This willingness is already evident in government institutions. Serious efforts are being pursued to advance legislation and to implement projects that will improve coastal management. Obviously, the next step is to engage in a broader dialogue that permits discussion of this Vision, and adoption of it after appropriate modification within the context of global, regional, national and local realities.

The greatest challenges will lie within Tanzania and Zanzibar themselves. For Blueprint 2050 to be realized, political commitment to a number of complementary near-term actions is required.

Ecology

- Improving our scientific knowledge base must receive highest priority. The near-term development of a national biogeographical classification would contribute significantly to addressing some of the knowledge gaps.

- Formalizing institutional arrangements for information management within URT is required.

Poverty alleviation

- Replication of successful models of community-based enterprise development, through ecologically and culturally appropriate alternative income generation, holds the greatest promise.

- Awareness-building and education efforts – related to sustainable use, management and protection of marine and coastal resources – will contribute meaningfully to poverty reduction and local empowerment.

Financing

- Efforts are already underway to improve revenues and reduce costs at many sites. Increased attention to revenue sharing is needed, both at individual sites (through clarifying retention mechanisms or co-management arrangements) and among sites.

- A risk pooling mechanism – such as a Marine Legacy Fund – should receive renewed attention.

Institutions

- Legislative reform continues apace as URT continues to decentralize many obligations and responsibilities. The single most important institutional and legal aspect within the context of Blueprint 2050 will be to clarify and entrench the rights and responsibilities of coastal communities. A cornerstone to this is the establishment of a community territorial sea, with explicit management rights conferred to coastal districts.

All of the above priority near-term actions will need to be wrapped together in a transparent and inclusive process that respects the contributions of all potential stakeholders. As a starting point, the concepts and ideas expressed in this document need to be placed through a broader dialog, with modifications where necessary and appropriate. As specific elements receive wider acceptance, they can be further entrenched in policies or legislation, and implemented through specific actions.

Monitoring failures and successes along the way is an important part of realizing the long-term Vision in Blueprint 2050. To achieve the long-term Vision, the adaptive processes will learn from the failures and will replicate and build on the successes. Over the coming decades, we should also be able to detect generally positive trends. For example, the current level of protection is less than 4 percent of the territorial sea; Blueprint 2050 calls for long-term effective management of about 40 percent and the URT has committed to targets of 10 percent by 2012 and 20 percent by 2025.

A Closing Word

In closing, we wish to give the final word to a key stakeholder who has – through both legal and moral right – the interests of the entire country at heart. The Ministry of Foreign Affairs is entrusted with the management and care of Tanzania's and Zanzibar's exclusive economic zone. The EEZ extends from the low waterline or baseline mark, to a maximum outer limit of 200 nautical miles. In April 2004, we had the pleasure of conducting an interview with Mr Philemon Luhanjo, Permanent Secretary of the Ministry of Foreign Affairs, during which we outlined the Blueprint 2050 Vision. In closing, he had this to say:

 The importance of managing this entire area is recognized in the Act; management in the deep sea is especially critical. Increasing revenues will be the key to poverty reduction in coastal areas, as well as in the country as a whole. The Ministry of Foreign Affairs only has a coordinating role; implementation will be by sectors – whether fisheries, oil and gas, transport, or others. We will have to work together to determine the best methods of management, and capacity building will be needed at all levels.

Endnotes

As noted in the Preface, this book is based on a series of scientific and technical studies conducted in 2003 and 2004. While Chapter 1 provides a synopsis of all of the other chapters, each subsequent chapter relies to varying degrees on findings from these background studies. Chapter 2 on ecological aspects is taken partly from Wells et al. (2004). Chapter 3 on poverty alleviation relies on summaries of León et al. (2003) and Silva et al. (2004), as well as on content on cultural issues derived from Moon (2004). Chapter 4 relies on background information from Hurd et al. (2003) and Lindhjem et al. (2003). The legal and institutional aspects summarized in Chapter 5 rely on Shauri (2003). Unless specifically attributed to an individual, the "conversations" in this book are fictitious and are not attributable to any one person; they are constructed by the editors based on background information and on feedback received during the peer review process.

Chapter 1

1.1   The reader is cautioned that different authors use different baselines for calculating the percentage of marine area under effective protection or management. The actual government commitment cited at the opening of this chapter (10 percent by 2012, 20 percent by 2025) did not provide a baseline. For this study, we use the convention of calculating the percentage as a proportion of the territorial seas (as opposed to continental shelf, EEZ, or measures depending on high tide marks instead of low tide marks).

1.2   The coelacanth story is summarized from an article entitled "Latest Coelacanth Discovery" that appeared in October 2003 at http://www.scienceinafrica.co.za/, which is the website for "Science in Africa: Africa's First On-Line Science Magazine."

1.3   Some opening and closing quotes in Chapter 1 and Chapter 6 are taken from the transcript of Finding Nemo, which is copyright 2003 Walt Disney Pictures and Pixar Animation Studios, and contains parts of a screenplay written by Andrew Stanton, Bob Peterson and David Reynolds. The transcript is property of Andrew Stanton, Bob Peterson and David Reynolds, Walt Disney Pictures and Pixar Animation Studios.

Chapter 2

2.1   The opening quote in this chapter refers to some of the earlier writings on systems analysis within complex or chaotic systems. The quote from John Gall comes from: Gall J. 1978. Systemantics: How Systems Really Work and How They Fail. Pocket Books, New York.

Chapter 3

3.1   This chapter covers a number of different poverty measures, and summarizes results from various surveys and sources. The reader is cautioned that – because of the nature of poverty measures – some of the measurements themselves may be problematic. For example, surveys elsewhere have shown that the poorest of the poor may be excluded from such surveys, or may be improperly represented. To be reliable, some measures (such as food poverty measures) require very detailed survey work. Benchmarks (such as the "dollar a day" measure) may also be biased if there have been dramatic exchange rate movements. As a consequence, poverty trends are often more meaningful than single poverty measures for specific sites or specific years. Similarly, comparisons between surveys can be problematic if they use different measurement samples or techniques. Reconciling all of these factors is beyond the scope of this book. But significant methodological and practical work has been on-going in Tanzania since about 2000, which is when the government's Poverty Reduction Strategy Paper (PRSP) was released. The PRSP is a medium term strategy to reduce poverty, promoting a range of poverty focused activities that will have a sustainable impact on poverty reduction in Tanzania. The reader is referred to up-to-date progress on poverty measurement in Tanzania at the Government's website (http://www.povertymonitoring.go.tz/); a comprehensive review of the PRSP will be undertaken during 2004 to update the process and make it more comprehensive. For a recent report, the reader is referred to: URT, 2004 (March). "Poverty Reduction Strategy: The Third Progress Report 2002/03," Dar es Salaam.

3.2   Additional discussion of complex systems and adaptive management possibilities can be found in a paper by Jack Ruitenbeek and Cynthia Cartier, entitled "Invisible Wand: Adaptive Co-management as an Emergent Strategy in Complex Bio-economic Systems", published in 2001 by the Center for International Forestry Research, Bogor.

Chapter 4

4.1   The opening quote in this chapter is taken from Oscar Wilde, 1912, *The Model Millionaire*. In accordance with Wilde's intent, and consistent with some of the literature on poverty reduction that focuses on cash incomes, we take the meaning of "permanent income" to be one of *actual* financial flows. This may be different from the "permanent income" with which some students of neoclassical economics may be familiar. Milton Friedman received a Nobel prize in 1976 for his work on consumption functions (inter alia), of which his *Permanent Income Hypothesis* formed a part. In Friedman's construct, consumption decisions would be based on a permanent income which is what an individual *presumed* she would earn throughout her life. The actual earnings could (and would likely) differ from this, being less than or more than this amount as circumstances changed from month to month or from year to year. Therefore, Friedman's meaning of permanent income is more of a concept: it is the annualized equivalent of a flow of income that can be expected to vary over time. Our use of "permanent income" is similar to this, but it is the actual (rather than conceptual) cash amount.

4.2   Visitor numbers are cited as being "over 500 000 annually" from 2000 to 2003. Actual figures – from the World Tourism Organization, *Tourism Fact Book: United Republic of Tanzania* – show inbound visitors to be 501 000 in 2000, 525 000 in 2001, 575 000 in 2002, and 576 000 in 2003; this represents annual average growth of 4.8 percent over the period.

4.3   Our calculation of the impacts on electricity prices is based on the Songo Songo project description as appraised in 2001 and described in the Project Appraisal Document (World Bank Report No 21316-TA). Calculations are approximate and are based on 100% flow through of costs across the entire potential project capacity (although initial installed capacity is 112 MW, the gas production capacity is adequate for 270 MW).

Chapter 5

5.1   Cicero's statement that "The people's good is the highest law" is found in his De Legibus. A modern translation is available as Keyes CW. 1928. Cicero: De re Publica, de Legibus. Harvard University Press, Cambridge, 544 pp, ISBN 0674992350.

5.2   The statement "… we seem to have a legal situation where both Tanzania (sic) and Zanzibar may declare protected areas independently, and where there is no legal terminology that is binding for both parts of the Union" is attributed to Sybille Riedmiller (Project Director, Chumbe Island Coral Park Ltd.) in Shauri's 2003 background study.

5.3   We note that enforcement in the EEZ is slowly improving as a consequence of recent expansion of Monitoring, Control and Surveillance (MCS) efforts sponsored by the European Union. The first large fishing operator was successfully prosecuted – in 2004 – for illegal fishing as a consequence of surveillance evidence. Also, Navy cooperation with local authorities is credited by some with decreasing illegal efforts within the Tanga management area.

5.4   The extracts from Grotius's *Mare Liberum* dissertation in this chapter are accessible in full in the following translation: Magoffin R. 2000. Originally released as "Hugo Grotius. 1633. The Freedom of the Seas or the Right Which Belongs to the Dutch to Take Part in the East Indian Trade: a Dissertation by Hugo Grotius, Translated with a Revision of the Latin Text of 1633 by Ralph Van Deman Magoffin, PhD, Associate Professor of Greek and Roman History. 1916 The Johns Hopkins Press." Batoche Books Limited, Kitchener, ISBN 1-55273-048-4.

Chapter 6

6.1   The saying "Ukiona vyaelea vimeundwa: When you see vessels afloat, somebody made them" has the metaphorical meaning "Nothing comes out of nothing! One has to work for whatever he or she wishes to achieve." This particular reference is attributed to a collection of khanga sayings compiled by Hassan Ali, Ottawa, Canada, 1995 entitled "Kanga Writings."

Sources

Andrew Hurd, Henrik Lindhjem, Jack Ruitenbeek. 2003 June. Sustainable Financing of Marine Protected Areas in Tanzania.

Yolanda León, James Tobey, Elin Torell, Rose Mwaipopo, Adolfo Mkenda, Zainab Ngazy, Farhat Mbarouk. 2004 February. MPAs and Poverty Alleviation: An Empirical Study of 24 Coastal Villages on Mainland Tanzania and Zanzibar.

Henrik Lindhjem, Andrew Hurd, Jack Ruitenbeek. 2003 June. Sustainable Financing of Marine Protected Areas in Zanzibar.

Karen Moon. 2004 April. Cultural Tourism on the Tanzanian Coast and Islands.

Vincent Shauri. 2003 October. Study on the Legal and Institutional Framework for Marine Conservation Areas in the United Republic of Tanzania.

Patricia Silva, Paavo Eliste, Adolfo Mkenda. 2004 February. Poverty Analysis of Coastal Communities in Tanzania.

Sue Wells, Saada Juma, Chris Muhando, Vedast Makota, Tundi Agardy. 2004 February. Study on the Ecological Basis for Establishing a System of MPAs and Marine Management Areas in the United Republic of Tanzania.

Chapter 2: Consolidated Sources from Wells at al. (2004)

Agardy T, Bridgewater P, Crosby MP, Day J, Dayton PK, Kenchington R, Laffoley D, McConney P, Murray PA, Parks JE, Peau L. 2003c. Dangerous targets: Differing perspectives, unresolved issues, and ideological clashes regarding marine protected areas. Aquatic Conservation: Marine and Freshwater Ecosystems 13:1-15.

Agardy T, Wolfe L. 2002. Institutional Options for Integrated Management of a North American Marine Protected Areas Network: Commission on Environmental Cooperation Report. CEC, Montreal.

Agardy T. 1997. Marine Protected Areas and Ocean Conservation. Academic Press, Dallas, Texas, USA.

Agardy T. 1999. Creating havens for marine life. Issues in Science and Technology Fall:37-44.

Agardy T. 2000. Effects of fisheries on marine ecosystems: a conservationist's perspective. ICES Journal of Marine Science 57:761-765.

Agardy T. 2003. An environmentalist's perspective on responsible fisheries: The need for holistic approaches. In: Sinclair M, Valdimarsson G. Eds. Responsible Fisheries in the Marine Ecosystem. CABI, UK

Agardy T. 2003. Optimal design of individual marine protected areas and MPA systems. Proceedings of the Conference on Aquatic Protected Areas, 8-12 August 2002, Cairns, Australia.

Airame S, Dugan J, Lafferty KD, Leslie H, McArdle DA, Warner RR. 2003. Applying ecological criteria to marine reserve design: a case study from the California Channel Islands. Ecological Applications 13 S:170-184.

Alder J. 1996. Have tropical marine protected areas worked? An initial analysis of their success. Coastal Management 24:97-114.

Allison G, Gaines S, Lubchenco J, Possingham H. 2003. Ensuring persistence of marine reserves: catastrophes require adopting an insurance factor. Ecological Applications 13 S:8-24.

Amir OA, Berggren D, Jiddawi NS. 2002. The incidental catch of dolphins in gillnet fisheries in Zanzibar, Tanzania. Western Indian Ocean Journal of Marine Science 1(2):155-161.

Andron JA, Lash J, Haggarty D. 2002. Modeling a Network of Marine Protected Areas for the Central Coast of British Columbia. Version 3.1. Living Oceans Society. Sointula BC, Canada.

ANZECC Task Force on Marine Protected Areas. 1998. Guidelines for establishing the National Representative System of Marine Protected Areas. In: Strategic Plan of Action for the National Representative System of Marine Protected Areas: a guide for action by Australian Governments. Environment Australia, Canberra.

Attwood CG. 2002. Spatial and temporal dynamics of exploited reef fish populations. PhD Thesis. University of Cape Town, South Africa. 299 pp.

Baker NE, Baker EM. 2002. Important Bird Areas in Tanzania: A First Inventory. Wildlife Conservation Society of Tanzania, Dar es Salaam, Tanzania.

Ballantine W. 1997. Design principles for systems of "no-take" marine reserves. In: The Design and Monitoring of Marine Reserves: 1-19. Fisheries Center, UBC, Vancouver, British Columbia

Bedward M, Pressey RL, Keith DA. 1992. A new approach for selecting fully representative reserve networks: addressing efficiency, reserve design and land suitability with an iterative analysis. Biological Conservation 62:115-125.

Bennett AF. 2003. Linkages in the Landscape: the role of corridors and connectivity in wildlife conservation. IUCN, Gland, Switzerland and Cambridge, UK. 254pp.

Board of Trustees Marine Parks and Reserves, Tanzania. 2000. Mafia Island Marine Park General Management Plan.

Brown K, Adger W, Tompkins E, Bacon P, Shim D, Young K. 2001. Trade-off analysis for marine protected area management. Ecological Economics 37:417-434.

Brown K, Tompkins E, Adger W. 2002. Making Waves: Integrating Coastal Conservation and Development. Earthscan, London.

Cappo M, Kelley R. 2000. Connectivity in the Great Barrier Reef World Heritage Area: an overview of pathways and processes. In: Wolankski E. Ed. Oceanographic Processes of Coral Reefs: Physical and Biological Links in the Great Barrier Reef. CRC Press:161-187.

Chernela JM, Ahmad A, Khalid F, Sinnamon V, Jaireth H. 2002. Innovative governance of fisheries and tourism in community-based protected areas. Parks 12(2):28-41.

Cooke A, Hamad AS. 1998. Misali Island Conservation Area, Pemba: Analysis of activities and lessons learned. In: Moffat D, Kyewalyanga M. Eds. Local community Integrated Coastal Zone Management: experiences from Eastern Africa. SEACAM/WIOMSA.

Cote I, Mosqueira I, Reynolds J. 2001. Effects of marine reserve characteristics on the protection of fish populations: a meta-analysis. Journal of Fish Biology 59 (SA):178-189.

Cowper D, Darwall WR. 1996. Sea turtles of the Songo Songo Islands. Miombo 15:14-15.

Curran S. 2002. Menai Bay Conservation Area Guidebook. WWF Tanzania. 51 pp.

Dahl A. 1993. The large marine ecosystem approach to regional seas action plans and conventions: A geographic perspective. Pp 15-17. In: Sherman K, Alexander L, Gold B. Eds. Large Marine Ecosystems: Stress, Mitigation, and Sustainability. AAAS Press, Washington DC.

Darwall WRT, Guard M. 2000. Southern Tanzania. Chapter 5. In: McClanahan TR, Sheppard CRC, Obura DO. Eds. Coral Reefs of the Indian Ocean: Their Ecology and Conservation. Oxford University Press, New York. Pp 131-165.

Davey AG. 1998. National System Planning for Protected Areas. IUCN, Gland, Switzerland and Cambridge, UK. 71pp.

Day JC, Fernandes L, Lewis A, De'Ath G, Slegers S, Barnett B, Keriigan B, Breen D, Innes J, Oliver J, Ward T, Lowe D. In press. The Representative Areas Program – protecting the biodiversity of the Great Barrier Reef World Heritage Area. Coral Reefs.

Day JC, Roff JC. 2000. Planning for Representative Marine Protected Areas: A Framework for Canada's Oceans. Report prepared for World Wildlife Fund Canada, Toronto.

Dayton P, Thrush S, Agardy T, Hofman R. 1995. Environmental effects of marine fishing. Aquatic Conservation: Marine and Freshwater Ecosystems 5:205-232.

De Fontaubert C, Downes D, Agardy T. 1996. Biodiversity in the Seas: Protecting Marine and Coastal Biodiversity and Living Resources Under the Convention on Biological Diversity. Island Press, Washington DC: 85pp

Done TJ. 2001. Scientific principles for establishing MPAs to alleviate coral bleaching and promote recovery. In: Salm RV, Coles SL. Eds. Coral Bleaching and Marine Protected Areas. Proceedings of the Workshop on Mitigating Coral Bleaching through MPA Design. Bishop Museum, Honolulu, Hawaii.

Dyer CL, McGoodwin JR. 1994. Introduction. In: Dyer CL, McGoodwin JR. Eds. Folk Management in the World's Fisheries: Lessons for Modern Fisheries Management. University of Colorado Press: Niwot:1-15

Fowler SL, Camhi M, Burgess GH, Cailliet GM, Fordham SV, Cavanagh RD, Simpfendorfer CA, Musick JA. In press. Sharks, rays and chimaeras: the status of the chondrichthyan fishes. IUCN SSC Shark Specialist Group. IUCN, Gland, Switzerland and Cambridge, UK.

Francis J, Mahongo S, Semesi A. 2001. Part 1. The Coastal Environment. In: Eastern Africa Atlas of Coastal Resources. UNEP.

Francis J, Wagner GM, Mvungi A, Ngwale J, Sallema R. 2001. Tanzania National Report, Phase I: Integrated Problem Analysis. GEF MSP Sub-Saharan Africa Project on Development and Protection of the Coastal and Marine Environment in Sub-Saharan Africa. 60pp.

Gardner TA, Cote IM, Gill JA, Grant A, Watkinson AR. 2003. Long-term region-wide declines in Caribbean corals. Science Express report; published on line 17 July 2003; 10.1126/science.1086050. www.sciencemag.org.

Gell FR, Roberts CM. 2003. Benefits beyond boundaries: the fishery effects of marine reserves. Trends in Ecology and Evolution 18(9):448-455.

Grantham BA, Eckert GL, Shanks AL. 2003. Dispersal potential of marine invertebrates in diverse habitats. Ecological Applications 13 S:108-116.

Green E. 2003. World Atlas of Sea Grasses, UNEP – World Conservation Monitoring Centre, Cambridge, UK.

Gwynne MD, Parker ISC, Wood DG. 1970. Latham Island: an ecological note. The Geographical Journal 136:247-251.

Halpern BS. 2003. The impact of marine reserves: do reserves work and does reserve size matter? Ecological Applications 13 S:117-137.

Halpern BS, Warner RR. 2002. Marine reserves have rapid and lasting effects. Ecology Letters 5:361-366.

Hansen L. 2003. Increasing the resistance and resilience of tropical marine ecosystems to climate change. In: Hansen LJ, Biringer JL, Hoffman JR. Eds. Buying Time: A User's Manual for Building Resistance and Resilience to Climate Change in Natural Systems. WWF, USA. Pp 155-174.

Hanson AJ, Agardy T, Perez G, Salcido R. 2000. Securing the Continent's Biological Wealth: Toward Effective Biodiversity Conservation in North America. Commission on Environmental Cooperation Report. CEC, Montreal.

Hillary A, Kokkonen M, Max L. 2003. Proceedings of the World Heritage Marine Biodiversity Workshop. Hanoi, Vietnam, Feb 25- March 1, 2002.

Hockey PAR, Branch GM. 1997. Criteria, objectives and methodology for evaluating marine protected areas in South Africa. South African Journal of Marine Science 18:369-383.

Horrill JC, Kalombo H, Makoloweka S. 2001. Collaborative Reef and Reef Fisheries Management in Tanga, Tanzania. Tanga Coastal Zone Conservation and Development Programme, IUCN Eastern Africa Programme, Nairobi, Kenya.

Horrill JC, Kamukuru AT, Mgaya YD, Risk M. 2000. Northern Tanzania and Zanzibar. Chapter 6. In: McClanahan TR, Sheppard CRC, Obura DO. Eds. Coral Reefs of the Indian Ocean: Their Ecology and Conservation. Oxford University Press, New York. Pp 131-165.

Horsfall IM. 1998. Sea cucumbers in Tanzania. Miombo 18:4-5.

Howell KM, Semesi AK. Eds. 1999. Coastal Resources of Bagamoyo District, Tanzania. Proc. Workshop on Coastal Resources of Bagamoyo, 18-19 Dec 1997. Faculty of Science, Univ. Dar es Salaam. 156pp.

Jackson JBC, Kirby MX, Berger WH, Bjorndal KA, Botsford LW, Bourque BJ, Bradbury RH, Cooke R, Erlandson J, Estes JA, Hughes TP, Kidwell S, Lange CB, Lenihan HS, Pandolfi JM, Petersen CH, Steneck RS, Tegner MJ, Warner RR. 2001. Historical overfishing and the recent collapse of coastal ecosystems. Science 293:629-638.

Jentoft S, McCay B. 1995. User participation in fisheries management, lessons drawn from international experiences. Marine Policy 19(3):227-246.

Jiddawi NS, Khatib AA. 2002. Sea turtle management in Zanzibar. Paper presented in the Faculty of Science Workshop. Dar es Salaam.

Jiddawi NS, Ohman MC. 2002. Marine fisheries in Tanzania. Ambio 31(7-8):518-527.

Jiddawi NS, Yahya SAS. 2003. Zanzibar Fisheries Frame Survey 2003. Department of Fisheries and Marine Resources, Zanzibar.

Jones PJS. 1994. A review and analysis of the objectives of marine nature reserves. Ocean and Coastal Management 23(3):149-178.

Kelleher G, Bleakley C, Wells S. Eds. 1995. A Globally Representative System of Marine Protected Areas. Vol 1. The Great Barrier Reef Marine Authority, The World Bank, and IUCN. World Bank, Washington DC, USA.

Kelleher G, Kenchington R. 1992. Guidelines for Establishing Marine Protected Areas. A Marine Conservation and Development Report. IUCN, Gland, Switzerland. 79pp.

Kithakeni T, Ndaro SGM. 2002. Some aspects of sea cucumber Holothuria scabra (Jaeger, 1935) along the coast of Dar es Salaam. Western Indian Ocean Journal of Marine Sciences 1(2):163-168.

Kramer DL, Chapman MR. 1999. Implications of fish home range size and relocation for marine reserve function. Environmental Biology of Fishes 55:65-79.

Lauck T, Clark CW, Mangel M, Munro GR. 1998. Implementing the precautionary principle in fisheries management through marine reserves. Ecological Applications 8 S:72-78.

Leslie H, Rucklehaus M, Ball I, Andelman S, Possingham H. 2003. Using siting algorithms in the design of marine reserve networks. Ecological Applications 13 S:185-198.

Lockwood D, Hastings A, Botsford L. 2002. The effects of dispersal patterns on marine reserves: does the tail wag the dog? Theoretical Population Biology 61:297-309.

Lubchenco J, Palumbi S, Gaines S, Andelman S. 2003. Plugging a hole in the ocean: the emerging science of marine reserves. Ecological Applications 13 S:3-7.

Mallella J, Gallop K, Guard M. 1999. Seahorses of southern Tanzania. Miombo Quarterly Magazine of the Wildlife Conservation Society of Tanzania.

Margules CR, Cresswell ID, Nicholls AO. 1994. A scientific basis for establishing networks of protected areas. In: Forey PL, Humphries CJ, Vane-Wright RI. Eds. Systematics and Conservation Evaluation. Clarendon Press, Oxford, UK. Pp 327-350.

Marshall NT, Barnett R. Eds. 1997. The Trade in Sharks and Shark Products in the Western India and Southest Atlantic Oceans. TRAFFIC International. Cambridge, UK.

McClanahan TR, Muthiga NA, Kamukuru AT, Machano H, Kiambo RW. 1999. The effects of marine parks and fishing on the coral reefs of northern Tanzanian. Biological Conservation 89:161-182.

Mgaya Y, Juma S. 2001. Integrated Coastal Zone Management in Tanzania. Pp.123-143. In: Voabil C, Engdahl S. Eds. The Voyage from Seychelles to Maputo: successes and failures of integrated coastal zone management in Eastern Africa and island states, 1996-2001. Vol. 1. Eastern African mainland country and regional reports. SEACAM, Maputo, Mozambique.

Mohammed SM, Muhando CA, Machano H. 2002. Coral reef degradation in Tanzania: Results of Monitoring 1999-2002. In: Linden O, Souter D, Wilhelmsson D, Obura D. Eds. Coral Reef Degradation in the Indian Ocean, Status Report 2002. CORDIO, Kalmar, Sweden.

Morgan J. 1989. Large marine ecosystems in the Pacific Ocean. Pp 377-394. In: Sherman K, Alexander L. Eds. Biomass Yields and Geography of LMEs. Westview Press, Boulder, Colo.

Morgan L, Etnoyer P, Wilkinson T, Herrmann H, Tsao F. 2003. Identifying priority conservation areas from Baja California to the Bering Sea. In: Making Ecosystem-based Management Work. Proceedings of the Fifth International Conference on Science and Management of Protected Areas, 11-16 May 2003, Victoria, Canada.

Muhando CA, Mohammed MS. 2002. Coral reef benthos and fisheries in Tanzania before and after the 1998 bleaching and mortality event. Western Indian Ocean Journal of Marine Sciences 1(1):43-52.

Muir CE, Abdallah O. 2002. Community based Marine Turtles and Dugong Research and habitat protection programme. Mafia Island Progress Report.

Muir CE, Sallema A, Abdallah O, De Luca D, Davenport,TRB. 2003. The dugong (Dugong dogon) in Tanzania: a national assessment of status, distribution and threat. WCS/WWF. 24pp.

Muir CE. 2002. The Mafia Island Turtles and Dugong Conservation programme. In Tanzania Marine Parks and Reserve Newsletter 1 January-June, p4.

Mumby PJ, et al. 2004. Mangroves enhance the biomass of coral reef fish communities in the Caribbean. Nature 427:533-536.

Myers RA, Worm B. 2003. Rapid worldwide depletion of predatory fish communities. Nature 423:280-283.

Nassor M. 1998. National perspective of management of marine protected areas in Zanzibar. In: Salm RV, Tessema,Y. Eds. Partnership for Conservation: Report of the Regional Workshop on Marine Protected Areas, Tourism and Communities. Diani Beach, Kenya, 11-13 May, 1998. IUCN Eastern African Regional Office, Nairobi, Kenya. Pp 46-49.

National Research Council. 2001. Marine Protected Areas: Tools for Sustaining Ocean Ecosystems. Committee on the Evaluation, Design and monitoring of marine reserves and protected areas in the United States. Ocean Studies Board, National Research Council, Washington DC, 288pp.

Nilsson P. 1998. Criteria for the selection of marine protected areas. Report 4834. Swedish Environmental Protection Agency, Stockholm, Sweden.

Palumbi S, Gaines S, Andelman S. 2003. Plugging a hole in the ocean: the emerging science of marine reserves. Ecological Applications 13, S:185-198.

Parrish R. 1999. Marine reserves for fisheries management: why not? California Cooperative Oceanic Fisheries Investigation Report 40:77-86.

Pauly D, Christensen V, Guenette S, Pichter TJ, Sumaila UR, Walters CJ, Watson R, Zeller D. 2002. Towards sustainability in world fisheries. Nature 418:689-695.

Possingham H, Ball I, Andelman S. 2000. Mathematical models for identifying representative reserve networks. In Ferson S, Burgman MA. Eds. Quantitative Methods in Conservation Biology:291-306. Springer-Verlag, NY.

Prescott V. 1993. Role of national political factors in the management of LMEs: evidence from West Africa. Pp 280-291 in Sherman K, Alexander L, Gold B. Eds. Large Marine Ecosystems: Stress, Mitigation, and Sustainability. AAAS Press, Washington DC

Pressey RL, Humphries CJ, Margules CR, Vane-Wright RI, Williams PH. 1993. Beyond opportunism: key principles for systematic reserve selection. Trends in Ecology and Evolution 8(4):124-128.

Ray C. 1968. Marine Parks for Tanzania. Results of a survey of the coast of Tanzania. Conservation Foundation. New York Zoological Society.

Revolutionary Government of Zanzibar. 1993. Tourism Zoning Plan. Zanzibar Integrated Land and Environmental Managed Project. Finnish International Development Agency – National Board of Survey, 52pp.

Richmond MD, Wilson JDK, Mgaya YD, Le Vay L. 2002. An analysis of small holder opportunities in fisheries, coastal and related enterprises in the floodplain and delta areas of the Rufiji River, Tanzania. Rufiji Environment Management Project Technical Report 25. IUCN Eastern Africa Regional Office, Nairobi, Kenya. 98pp.

Roberts CM, Branch G. Bustamente RH, Castilla JC, Dugan J, Halpern BS, Lafferty KD, Leslie H, Lubchenco J, McArdle S, Ruckelshaus M, Warner RR. 2003a. Ecological criteria for evaluating candidate sites for marine reserves. Ecological Applications 13(1) S:199-214.

Roberts CM, Branch G. Bustamente RH, Castilla JC, Dugan J, Halpern BS, Lafferty KD, Leslie H, Lubchenco J, McArdle S, Ruckelshaus M, Warner RR. 2003b. Application of ecological criteria in selecting marine reserves and developing reserve networks. Ecological Applications 13(1) S:215-228.

Roberts CM, Halpern B, Palumbi SR, Warner RR. 2001. Designing marine reserve networks: Why small, isolated protected areas are not enough. Conservation Biology in Practice 2(3):12-19.

Roberts CM, Hawkins J. 1999. Extinction risk in the sea. Trends in Ecology and Evolution 14:241-246.

Roberts CM, Hawkins J. 2000. Fully Protected Marine Reserves: a Guide. World Wildlife Fund, Washington DC.

Roberts CM, McClean CJ, Veron JEN, Hawkins JP, Allen GR, McAllister DE, Mittermeier CG, Schueler FW, Spalding M, Wells F, Vynne C, Werner T. 2002. Marine biodiversity hotspots and conservation priorities for tropical reefs. Science 295:1280-1284.

Roberts CM. 2003. Our shifting perspectives on the oceans. Oryx 37(2):166-177.

Roxburgh T, Morton I, Rumisha C, Francis J. Eds. 2002. An assessment of the stakeholders and resource use in the Dar es Salaam Marine Reserves System. International Coral Reef Action Network (ICRAN) and Wesstern Indian Ocean Marine Science Association (WIOMSA).

Ruddle K. 1988. Social principles underlying traditional inshore fishery management systems in the Pacific Basin. Marine Resource Economics 5:351-363.

Salm RV, Clark JR, Siirila E. 2000. Marine and Coastal Protected Areas: A Guide for Planners and Managers. IUCN, Washington D.C., USA. 371pp.

Salm RV, Coles SL. Eds. 2001. Coral Bleaching and Marine Protected Areas. Proc. Workshop on Mitigating Bleaching Impact through MPA Design. Bishop Museum, Honolulu, Hawaii, USA. 118pp, (doc available from: www. conserveonline.org).

Salm RV, et al. 2003. Bleaching toolkit.

Salm RV, Smith SE, Llewellyn G. 2001. Mitigating the impact of coral bleaching through marine protected area design. In: Schuttenberg HZ. Ed. Coral Bleaching: Causes, Consequences and Response. Coastal Management Report 2230. Coastal Resources Center, Univ. Rhode Island. 102pp.

Semesi AK Mzava EM. 1991. Management plans for mangrove ecosystem of mainland Tanzania. Vol 1-10. Ministry of Tourism Natural Resources and Environment, Forestry and beekeeping Division, Mangrove Management Project, Dar es Salaam.

Shanks AL, Grantham BA, Carr MH. 2001. Propagule dispersal distance and the size and spacing of marine reserves. Ecological Applications 13:S:159-169.

Sherman K. 1993. Large Marine Ecosystems as global units for marine resources management – an ecological perspective. In Sherman K, Alexander L, Gold B. Eds. Large Marine Ecosystems. AAAS Press, Washington DC. Pp 3-14.

Shumba. 1996. Mangroves on Unguja.

Spalding MD, Ravilious C, Green EP. 2001. World Atlas of Coral Reefs. UNEP-WCMC/ University of California Press.

Stensland E, Berggren E, Johnstone R, Jiddawi NS. 1998. Marine mammals in Tanzanian waters: urgent need for status assessment. Ambio 26(8):771-774.

Sumaila UR, Guenette S, Adler J, Chuenpagdee R. 2000. Addressing ecosystem effects of fishing using marine protected areas. ICES Journal of Marine Sciences 57:752-760.

Tanzania Coastal Management Partnership. 2001. State of the coastal survey.

Tanzania Coastal Management Partnership. 2003. National Integrated Coastal Environment Management Strategy. Tanzania Coastal Management Partnership, Dar es Salaam, Tanzania. 52pp.

Torell E, Luhikula G, Nzali LM. 2002. Managing Tanzania's coast through integrated planning: reflection upon the first year of the district ICM action planning. Tanzania Coastal Management Partnership, Dar es Salaam, Tanzania. 17pp.

United Republic of Tanzania. 2002. Tourism Master Plan. Strategy and Actions. Final Summary Update. Ministry of Natural Resources and Tourism.

US Federal Register. 2000. Presidential Documents, Executive Order 13158 of May 26, 2000. Vol. 65, No. 105. US Government Printing Office, Washington DC.

Villa F, Tunesi L, Agardy T. 2002. Zoning marine protected areas through spatial multiple-criteria analysis: the case of the Asinara Island National Marine Reserve of Italy. Conservation Biology 16(2):515-526.

Wagner G. 2003. State of the Coast 2003. Unpub. Report as a contribution to the TCMP State of the Coast Report.

Wang YQ, Ngusaru A, Tobey J, Bonynge G, Nugranad J, Makota V, Traber M. 2003. Remote sensing of mangrove change along the Tanzania coast. Marine Geodesy 26:35-48.

Ward T, Hegerl E. 2003. Marine Protected Areas in Ecosystem-based management of fisheries. Report to Dept. Environment and Heritage, Commonwealth of Australia. 66pp.

Ward T, Heinemann D, Evans N. 2002. The Role of Marine Reserves as Fisheries Management Tools. Bureau of Rural Sciences, Canberra 192pp.

Ward T, Vanderklift MA, Nicholls AO, Kenchington RA. 1999. Selecting marine reserves using habitats and species assemblages as surrogates for biological diversity. Ecological Applications 9:691-698.

Wells S. 2003. Developing the Eastern African Marine Ecoregion marine protected area network: progress made and actions needed in Kenya, Tanzania and Mozambique. Report to WWF Eastern African Marine Ecoregion Programme, Dar es Salaam, Tanzania.

West JM, Salm RV. 2003. Resistance and resilience to coral bleaching: Implications for coral reef conservation and management. Conservation Biology 17(4): 956-967.

Westmacott S, Teleki, Wells S. 2000. Bleaching manual.

Whitney A. Bayer, T. Daffa, J. Mahika, C. Tobe, J. 2003. Tanzania State of the Coastal Report 2003.Tanzania Coastal Management Partnership, Coastal Management Report #2002 TCMP, Dar es Salaam.

Wilkinson T, Agardy T, Perry S, Rojas L, Hyrenbach D, Morgan K, Fraser D, Janishevski L, Herrmann H, de la Cueva H. 2003. Marine species of common conservation concern: protecting species at risk across international boundaries. In: Making Ecosystem-based Management Work. Proceedings of the Fifth International Conference on Science and Management of Protected Areas, 11-16 May 2003, Victoria, Canada.

Zacharias MA, Roff JC. 2000. A hierarchical ecological approach to conserving marine biodiversity. Conservation Biology 14(5):1327-1334.

Zacharias MA, Roff JC. 2001. Use of focal species in marine conservation and management: a review and critique. Aquatic Conservation: Marine and Freshwater Ecosystems 11:59-76.

Chapter 3: Consolidated Sources from León et al. (2003)

Alder J. 1996. Have tropical marine protected areas worked? An initial analysis of their success. Coastal Management 24:97-114.

Ambler J. 1999. Attacking Poverty While Protecting the Environment: Toward Win-Win Policy Options. Poverty and Environment Initiative. UNDP, New York.

Asseid, B. 2000. Revisiting Ecological Behaviors of the Coastal Communities of Zanzibar: Implications for Non-formal Environmental Education Programs. PhD thesis submitted to the University of Reading, Department of Agricultural Extension and Rural Development.

Berkes F, Mahon R, McConney P, Pollnac R, Pomeroy R. 2001. Managing Small-scale Fisheries: Alternative Directions and Methods. International Development Research Centre, Ottawa, Canada.

Boersma P, Parrish J. 1999. Limiting abuse: Marine protected areas, a limited solution. Ecological Economics 31:287-304.

Brandon K, Redford K, Sanderson S. Eds. 1998. Parks in Peril: People, Politics, and Protected Areas. Island Press, Washington DC.

Brown K, Tompkins E, Adger W. 2002. Making Waves: Integrating Coastal Conservation and Development. Earthscan Publication Ltd., London and Sterling, VA.

Bunce L, Townsley P, Pomeroy R, Pollnac R. 2000. Socioeconomic Manual for Coral Reef Management. Australian Institute of Marine Science, Townsville, Australia.

Cicin-Sain B, Belfiore S. 2003. Linking marine protected areas to integrated coastal and ocean management: A review of theory and practice. Discussion Paper for CZ2003 and for the September 2003 World Parks Congress, prepared for NOAA and World Commission on Protected Areas.

Coastal Resource Management Project. 1998, Manage our coastal resources: Our food security will depend on it!, Coastal Resource Management Project, Philippines. Document No. 39-CRM/1998.

Crawford B, Balgos M, Pagdilao C. 2000. Community-based marine sanctuaries in the Philippines: A report on focus group discussions. Coastal Management Report #2224, PCAMRD Book 30, Coastal Resources Center and Philippine Council for Aquatic and Marine Research and Development, Narragansett, RI, USA, Los Banos, Laguna, Philippines.

Dulvy N, Stanwell-Smith D, Darwall W, Horrill C. 1995. Coral mining at Mafia Island, Tanzania: A management dilemma. Ambio 24:358-365.

FAO. 2000. Data on World Fisheries. FAO, Rome www.fao.org.

Gibbons P. 1997. The poor relation: A political economy of the marketing chain of dagaa in Tanzania. CDR Working Paper 97.2, June 1997. http://www.cdr.dk/working_papers/wp-97-2.htm

Guard M, Mgaya Y. 2002. The artisanal fishery of Octopus cyanea gray in Tanzania. Ambio 31(7-8):528-536.

Jiddawi N, Ohman M. 2002. Marine fisheries in Tanzania. Ambio 31(7-8):518-527.

Kelleher G. 1999. Guidelines for Marine Protected Areas. IUCN, Gland.

Kenchington R. 2000. Fisheries management and marine protected areas – A 2000 perspective. Intercoast Network, Newsletter of Coastal Management 37:4-5.

Kramer R, van Schaik C, Johnson J. 1997. Lessons from the Field: A Review of World Wildlife Fund's Experience with Integrated Conservation and Development Projects 1985-1996. Oxford University Press, New York.

Levine A. 2002. Global partnerships in Tanzania's marine resource management: NGOs, the private sector, and local communities. Manuscript. University of California, Berkeley, 14pp.

Masoud T. 2001. Linking conservation and community development: A case for Jozani-Chwaka Bay Conservation Project, Zanzibar. Manuscript. November, 12pp.

Narayan D. 1997, Voices of the poor: Poverty and social capital in Tanzania. Environmentally and Socially Sustainable Development Studies and Monographs Series 20, World Bank, Washington DC, 80pp.

National Bureau of Statistics. 2002. Household Budget Survey 2000/01. National Bureau of Statistics, Government of Tanzania, Dar es Salaam http://www.tanzania.go.tz/hbs/HomePage_HBS.html, accessed 4 December 2003.

Nations Development Programme /World Bank/EC/DFID. 2002. Linking poverty reduction and environmental management: Policy challenges and opportunities. A Contribution to the WSSD Process, Consultation Draft, January 2001.

Ngaga Y, Sharif M, Makoloweka S. 1999. Mid-term evaluation final report: Menai Bay Conservation Area. WWF Tanzania Program Office.

Oates J. 1999. Myth and Reality in the Rain Forest: How Conservation Strategies are Failing in West Africa. University of California Press, Berkeley, CA.

Pollnac R, Crawford B, Gorospe M. 2001. Discovering factors that influence the success of community-based marine protected areas in the Visayas, Philippines. Ocean and Coastal Management 44:683-710.

Pollnac R. 1998. Rapid Assessment of Management Parameters for Coral Reefs. ICLARM Contribution #1445, Coastal Management Report #2205. Coastal Resources Center, University of Rhode Island.

Pomeroy R, Parks J, Watson L. 2002. How is Your MPA doing? A guidebook. IUCN World Commission on Protected Areas WCPA and World Wide Fund for Nature WWF International MPA Management Effectiveness Initiative. Working Draft, 31 December.

Richmond M. Ed. 1997. A guide to the seashores of eastern Africa and the western Indian Ocean Islands. SIDA. 448pp.

Riedmiller S. 2000. Private sector management of marine protected area: The Chumbe Island Case, in Cesar H. Ed. Collected Essays on the Economics of Coral Reefs. CORDIO, Sida/SAREC Marine Science Program, Stockholm.

Spalding M, Ravilious C, Green E. 2001. World Atlas of Coral Reefs. UNEP World Conservation Monitoring Centre, University of California Press, Berkeley, 424pp.

Sterner T, Andersson J. 1998. Private protection of the marine environment, Tanzania: A case study. Ambio 27(8):768-771.

Tanzania Coastal Management Partnership. 2001. Tanzania State of the Coast 2001: People and the Environment. Coastal Management Report #2000 TCMP, Dar es Salaam, October.

Tanzania Coastal Management Partnership. 2003. Tanzania State of the Coast 2001: The National ICM Strategy and Prospects for Poverty Reduction. Coastal Management Report #2002 TCMP, Dar es Salaam, August.

Terborgh J. 1999. Requiem for Nature. Island Press, Washington DC.

Torell E, Tobey J, van Ingen T. 2000. ICM Action Planning: Lessons Learned from the Tanga Coastal Zone Conservation and Development Programme. Tanga. University of Rhode Island's Coastal Resources Center Tanga Coastal Zone Conservation and Development Programme.

United Nations Development Programme. 1999. A Better Life… With Nature's Help. Attacking Poverty While Improving the Environment: Practical Recommendations. Poverty and Environment Initiative, UNDP, New York.

Wang YQ, Tobey J, Bonynge G, Nugranad J, Makota V, Ngusaru A, Traber M. 2003. Remote sensing of land-cover change along the Tanzania coast for integrated coastal management and sustainable development. Paper submitted for publication to the Journal of Coastal Management.

Whittingham E, Campbell J, Townsley P. 2003. Poverty and Reefs, Volume 1: Global Overview. DFID, IOC/UNESCO and IMM Ltd. Printed by UNESCO, Paris.

World Bank. 1999. Voices from the village: A comparative study of coastal resource management in the Pacific Islands. Pacific Islands Discussion Paper 9, World Bank, Washington DC.

Chapter 3: Consolidated Sources from Silva et al. (2004)

Collier P, Radwan S, Wangwe S, with Wagner A. 1990. Labour and Poverty in Rural Tanzania: Ujamaa and Rural Development in the United Republic of Tanzania. Clarendon Press, Oxford.

Deaton A. 1997. The Analysis of Household Surveys: A Microeconometric Approach to Development Policy. John Hopkins University Press.

Foster J, Greer J, Thorbecke E. 1984. A class of decomposable poverty measures. Econometrica 52:761-766.

Glewwe P. 1991. Investigating the determinants of household welfare in Côte d'Ivoire. Journal of Development Economics 35:307-337.

Ravallion M. 1992. Poverty comparisons: a guide to concepts and methods. World Bank LSMS Working Paper 88.

Chapter 4: Consolidated Sources from Hurd et al. (2003)

Andersson JEC, Ngazi Z. 1995. Marine Resource Use and the Establishment of a Marine Park: Mafia Island, Tanzania. Ambio 24(7-8), December.

Andrews G. 1998. Mafia Island Marine Park, Tanzania: Implications of Applying a Marine Park Paradigm in a Developing Country. ITMEMS Proceedings.

Board of Trustees, Marine Parks and Reserves. 2002. Draft Consolidated Financial Statements for the year ended 30th June 2002.

Dulvy NK, Stanwell-Smith D, Darwell WRT, Horrill CJ. 1995. Coral mining at Mafia Island, Tanzania: A management dilemma. Ambio 24(6), September.

Francis J, Nilsson A, Waruinge D. 2002. Marine Protected Areas in the Eastern African Region: How Successful Are They? Ambio 31(7-8), December.

Francis J, Wagner GM, Mvungi A, Ngwale J, Salema R. 2002. Tanzania National Report: Phase I – Problem Analysis as part of Development and Protection of the Coastal and Marine Environment in Sub-Saharan Africa. GEF. March.

Horrill JC, Darwall WRT, Ngoile M. 1996. Development of a Marine Protected Area: Mafia Island, Tanzania. Ambio 25(1), February.

Horrill JC. Feasibility of Improving District Revenues from the Fisheries Sector. Consultant report for the Tanga Program.

Horrill JC, Kalombo H, Makoloweka S. 2001. Collaborative Reef and Reef Fisheries Management in Tanga, Tanzania. IUCN Eastern Africa Regional Program. March.

Logsdon R. 1998. Revenue Collection, Tourism and Management of the MIMP. Consultant report for MPRU. May.

Mafia District Council. 2001. Taarifa ya Mapato na Matumizi kwa Januari hadi Disembra.

MIMP. 2002. Enforcement Costs – July 2001 – September 2002.

MIMP. 2002. Visitor and Fee Statistics at MIMP, 17 March – 31 December 2002.

MPRU, UNDP, IUCN. 2003. Development of Mnazi Bay – Ruvuma Estuary Marine Park: Inception Report. February.

MPRU. 2002. Financial Statements for MIMP (Branch of marine Parks and Reserves Tanzania) for the year ended 30th June 2002.

Nhwani, Rusumo. 2000. Report on the Economic and Financial Potentials of the MIMP's Marine Resources and the Best Way of Tapping them Sustainably. MPRU. August 2000.

Rusumo, Mkwavile, Kakuga. 2000. Economic and Financial Implications of the New Rates to Marine Parks and Reserves Revenue: Analysis of the Proposed New User Fee Tariffs. MNRT.

Tanga Municipal Council. Sheria Ndogo, Imetungwa chini ya Kifunga Na. 80.

Tanzania Coastal Management Partnership. 2000. Coastal Tourism Situation Analysis. Coastal Tourism Working Group.

Tanzania Coastal Management Partnership. 2002. Guidelines for District ICM Action Planning. Core Working Group.

URT, MNRT, Board of Trustees, Marine Parks and Reserves. 2001. Statement of Source and Application of Funds for the Year ended 30th June 2001.

URT. 2000. Conservation of Marine Resources and Environment Protection in Mafia Island Marine Park: Annual Progress Report for FY1999/2000. MNRT. July.

URT. 2000. Mafia Island Marine Park General Management Plan. September.

URT. 2000. Vice President's Office. GEF Project Proposal for Tanzania: Development of Mnazi Bay Marine Park.

URT. 2001. Conservation of Marine Resources and Environment Protection in Mafia Island Marine Park: Annual Progress Report for FY2000/2001. MNRT. July.

URT. 2001. Government Notice No. 232. Subsidiary Legislation to the Marine Parks and Reserves Act: Regulations. 21 September.

URT. 2001. Office of the Controller and Auditor General. Audited Accounts and Management Audit Report of the Financial Statements of the Marine Parks and Reserves Unit for the year ended 30th June 2001. September 2002, Dar es Salaam.

URT. 2002. Conservation of Marine Resources and Environment Protection in Mafia Island Marine Park: Annual Progress Report for FY2001/2002. MNRT. July.

URT. Conservation of Marine Resources and Environment Protection in Mafia Island Marine Park: Proposed Exit Strategy funding proposal for submission to NORAD. MNRT. April 2002.

URT. The Marine Parks and Reserves Act No. 29, 1994.

Van Ingen T, Kawau C, Wells S. 2002. Gender Equity in Coastal Zone Management: Experiences from Tanga, Tanzania. IUCN Eastern Africa Regional Program. December.

WWF UK. 2003. FY03 Revised Detailed Budget.

Chapter 4: Consolidated Sources from Lindhjem et al. (2003)

Abdullah A, Hama AS, Ali AM, Wild R. 2000. Misali Island, Tanzania – An open access resource redefined. Constituting the commons: Crafting sustainable commons in the new millennium. 8th biennial conference of the international association for the study of common property.

Abdullah HS, Kitwana M. 1997. Jozani – Chwaka Bay conservation area management plan. Zanzibar Forestry Technical Paper 96.

Baland, Platteau. 1996. Halting Degradation of Natural Resources. Is there a Role for Local Communities? Oxford: Clarendon Press.

Balmford A, Gravestock P, Hockley N, McClean C, Roberts C. 2003. The worldwide costs of marine conservation. Unpublished Working Paper.

CARE. 1996. Progress analysis of the Jozani Chwaka Bay Conservation Project.

CARE. 2002. Improving community livelihoods and conservation on Pemba. Final report to the Ford Foundation.

CARE. 2002a. Misali Island Conservation Project Review Workshop. Report on Proceedings and Results. May 4-7, 2002. Chake Chake, Pemba.

CARE. 2002b. Misali Island Conservation Project. Study Tour Trip to Kenya.

CHICOP. 1994a. Marine Sanctuary Agreement between the Ministry of Agriculture, Livestock and Natural Resources and Chumbe Island Coral Park Ltd.

CHICOP. 1994b. Closed Forest Agreement between the Ministry of Agriculture, Livestock, and Natural Resources and Chumbe Island Coral Park Limited.

CHICOP. 1995. Chumbe Island Coral Park. Marine Park and Forest Reserve. Management Plan 1995-2005. Flanking program for tropical ecology.

CHICOP. 1998. A Viability study [excerpts]. Determination of appropriate price structure for increased investment up to date.

CHL Consulting Group. 2002. Indicative Tourism Master Plan for Zanzibar. Consultation Draft October 2002.

CORDIO. 2002. Participatory Monitoring of Fisheries Resources in Pemba Misali – Training Workshop. October 2002.

DFMP. 1999. Kiwengwa Controlled Area. The proposed management plan.

DFMP. 2003. Various budgets and plans, revenue collection figures etc.

Ely A, Makame MK. 1998. Jozani – Chwaka Bay Conservation Project. Phase I. Final Report. Ministry of Agriculture, Livestock and Natural Resources. Forestry Technical Paper 103.

Francis J, Nilsson A, Waruinge D. 2002. Marine Protected Areas in the Eastern African Region: How successful are they? Ambio 317-8.

Francis J, Wagner GM, Mvungi A, Ngwale J, Salema R. 2002. Tanzania National Report. Phase 1: Integrated Problem Analysis. GEF Project: Development and protection of the Coastal and Marine Environment in Sub-Saharan Africa.

Geoghegan T, Smith AH, Smith K. 2001. Characterization of Caribbean Marine Protected Areas: An Analysis of Ecological, Organizational, and Socio-economic factors. CANARI Technical Report 287.

Gravestock P. 2002. Towards a better understanding of the income requirements of Marine Protected Areas. Unpublished MSc Thesis. Cranfield Uinversity.

IMS/CARE. 2002. Misali Island Environmental Monitoring. Coral reef monitoring.

James AN. 1999. Institutional constraints to protected area funding. Parks 92 June.

Kadu MA. 2001. Revenue collection information system for Menai Bay Conservation Area. Ministry of Agriculture, Natural Resources, Environment and Cooperatives. Department of Fisheries and Marine Products.

Khatib AA. 1996. Integrated coastal management initiatives at Chwaka Bay – Paje.

Lindberg K, Halpenny E. 2001. Protected Area Visitor Fees.

Machano H, Mohammed SM, Jiddawi NS. 2002. Coral reef fish populations monitoring. Second trip report. IMS/CARE report.

MacKinnon K 2001. Editorial Special Issue of Parks. ICDPs: working with parks and people.

Makame KM, Hamdan SI, Jumah SM. 2002. Management Plan for the Chwaka bay mangrove ecosystem 2003-2007. Forestry Technical Paper 135.

Malpas R, Mesaki S, Humphrey S. 2002. Menai Bay Conservation Area Project. Report of the Final Evaluation 16-26 June 2002.

Management Committee for Kiwengwa. 1999. Kiwengwa Controlled Area: Proposed Management Plan. Expected date of review: August 2002.

MANREC. 1989. Compensation agreement for the use of Mnemba island by the Archers Ltd.

MANREC. 1996. Operational Plan for 1997-1998. Menai Bay Conservation Area.

MANREC. 1998. Misali Island Marine Conservation and Forest Cutting Order. June.

MANREC. 1998. Operational Plan for FY 1999. Menai Bay Conservation Area

MANREC. 1999. Agricultural Sector Policy. Prepared by MANREC with the assistance of FAO. TCP/URT/6716.

MANREC. 1999. Operational Plan for FY 2000. Menai Bay Conservation Area.

MANREC. 1999. Report of the meeting to establish Mnemba advisory committee.

MANREC. 2000. Proposed activities for year 2001-2003. Menai Bay Conservation Area Commission for Natural Resources.

MANREC. 2001. Operation Plan FY. 2002. Menai Bay Conservation Area. Department of Fisheries and Marine Resources.

MANREC. 2002. Collection of revenue from visitors around Mnemba atoll conservation area. Letter to Tourist operators 4 November.

MANREC/WWF. 2001. Menai Bay Conservation Area General Management Plan in Kiswahili.

Misali Island Conservation Program. 2003. Various accounts, budgets and plans for MICA, DCCFF, CARE.

Mohammed SM. 1999. The ecology and socio-economy of Chwaka bay, Zanzibar. Report prepared for Jozani – Chwaka Bay Conservation Project. CARE, Tanzania. Supported by UNESCO and MAB.

Nasser SM. 1995. Socio-economic consideration of villages around Menai Bay, Zanzibar. In collaboration with Sub-commission of Fisheries, Department of Environment, Institute of Marine Science. Supporetd by WWF.

Riedmiller S. 1991. Chumbe Island Coral Park – educational snorkeling and diving center. Feasibility study.

Riedmiller S. 1998. The Chumbe Island Coral Park Project: Management Experiences of a private marine conservation project. ITMEM 1998 Proceedings.

Riedmiller S. 2000. Private sector management of marine protected areas: The Chumbe Island Case. In Cesar H. Ed. Collected Essays on the Economics of Coral Reefs. CORDIO/SIDA.

Shah A. 1995. The Economics of Third World National Parks. Edward Elgar.

Soley N. 1997. Chumbe Island Coral Park: Analysis of Costs. Paper presented at the Workshop on Revenue from nature conservation areas in Zanzibar 15-16 July.

Soley N. 1997. Socio-economic profile of the fisheries of Misali Island. The Environmnet and Development Group. Oxford.

Taylor M. 1998. Governing natural resources. Society and Natural Resources 11:251-258.

Wade R. 1987. The management of common property resources: collective action as an alternative to privatization or state regulation. Cambridge Journal of Economics 11:95-106

Westmacott S, Cesar H, Pet-Soede L, Linden O. 2000. Coral Bleaching in the Indian Ocean: Socio-economic assessment of effects. In Cesar H. Ed. Collected Essays on the Economics of Coral Reefs. CORDIO/SIDA

World Wide Fund for Nature. 1996. Support for community-based conservation and sustainable use of natural resources in Menai Bay, Zanzibar. Project Document. In collaboration with Sub-commission of Fisheries, Department of Environment, Institute of Marine Science.

Chapter 5: Consolidated Sources from Shauri (2003)

Hewawasam I. 2002. Managing the Marine and Coastal Environment of Sub-Saharan Africa: Strategic Directions for Sustainable Development. World Bank, Washington DC.

Makaramba R, Kweka O. 1999. Developing an Integrated Coastal Zone Management Policy for Tanzania: Institutional and Policy Matrix. TCMP, Dar es Salaam.

Mhina MV. 1999. The Wildlife Conservation Act, 1974 and Wildlife Policy Of Tanzania: A Commentary on International and Regional Instruments to which Tanzania is a Party. Paper presented to EPIQ/USAID Project, Dar es salaam, Tanzania.

Mlimuka AKIJ. 1995. The Influence of the 1982 United Nations Convention on the Law of the Sea on State Practice: The Case of the Tanzanian Legislation Establishing the Exclusive Economic Zone. Journal of Ocean Development and International Law 26.

Ngusaru AS, et al. 2001. Tanzania State of the Coast 2001. People and the Environment. Tanzania Coastal Management Partnership Science and Technical Working Group. Dar es Salaam.

Richmond M, Francis J. Eds. 2001. Marine Science Development in Tanzania and Eastern Africa. Proceedings of the 20th Anniversary Conference on Advances in Marine Science in Tanzania, WIOMSA, Dar es Salaam.

Roxburgh T, Morton I, Rumisha C, Francis J. Eds. 2002. An Assessment of the Stakeholders and Resource Use in Dar es salaam Marine Reserves System. ICRAN/WIOMSA.

Tanzania Coastal Management Partnership. 1999. Issues and proposed goals and objectives of a National Management Policy. Green Paper. URT Working Document: 5026 TCMP.

Tanzania Coastal Management Partnership. 1999. Options for a National Integrated Coastal Management Policy. Communications Unit, Dar es Salaam.

Torrell E, Luhikula G, Nzali LM. 2002. Managing Tanzania's Coastal through Integrated Planning: Reflection upon the First Year of District ICM Action Planning. TCMP- A joint initiative between NEMC, UORI/CRC & USAID.

URT. 2003. National Integrated Coastal Environment Management Strategy. Vice President's Office.

World Commission on Protected Areas. No date. Marine Protected Areas at www.acmt.tr/classes/files/40/ Environmental_Science_11_lecture.7apdf.

Photo: Paavo Eliste